Teacher Professional Learning
in an Age of Compliance

Professional Learning and Development in Schools and Higher Education

Volume 2

Series Editors

Christopher Day
School of Education, University of Nottingham, UK
Judyth Sachs
Macquarie University, Australia

Editorial Board

P. Blackmore
Kings College London, London, UK
M. Cochran-Smith
Lynch School of Education, Boston College, Chestnut Hill, USA
J. Furlong
Department of Education, University of Oxford, UK
A. Lieberman
The Carnegie Foundation for the Advancement of Teaching, Stanford, USA
J. Orrell
School of Education, Flinders University, Adelaide, Australia
C. Sugrue
Cambridge University, Cambridge, UK

Professional Learning and Development in Schools and Higher Education disseminates original, research informed writing on the connections between teacher learning and professionalism in schools and higher education. Global in their coverage, the texts deal with the problems and practices of the field in different national and international cultural, policy and practice contexts. The methodology employed encompasses a broad spectrum of conceptual, theoretical, philosophical and empirical research activities. The series explicitly encompasses both the fields of schools and higher education.

The subject areas covered by the series are: professional learning in schools; contexts for professional learning; professional learning in higher education; change; the (new) meanings of professionalism in schools and higher education; training and development in schools and higher education; the 'well-being' agenda in schools and higher education; autonomy, compliance and effectiveness in schools and higher education; principal leadership in schools and higher education; middle-level leadership in schools and higher education.

For other titles published in this series, go to
www.springer.com/series/7908

Susan Groundwater-Smith • Nicole Mockler

Teacher Professional Learning in an Age of Compliance

Mind the Gap

 Springer

Susan Groundwater-Smith
Faculty of Education & Social Work
University of Sydney
NSW 2007
Australia

Nicole Mockler
School of Education
University of Newcastle
NSW 2258
Australia

ISBN 978-1-4020-9416-3   e-ISBN 978-1-4020-9417-0
DOI: 10.1007/978-1-4020-9417-0

Library of Congress Control Number: 2008944206

Printed on acid-free paper

springer.com

Preface

Alvin Toffler is credited with having written that the illiterate of the twenty-first century will not be those who cannot read and write but those who cannot learn, unlearn and relearn. Slightly amended the series of books under my own and Christopher Day's editorship could read, the de-professionalized teachers of the twenty first century will not be those who do not have an initial entry credential from a worthy tertiary institution, but those who see this as the end point of their professional learning and are not ready to further learn, unlearn and relearn their practice.

In our series *Professional Learning and Development in Schools and Higher Education* we proposed that our principal objective was to disseminate original, research-informed but 'readerly' writing to audiences of academics, teacher educators and leaders in schools and higher education. *Teacher Professional Learning in an Age of Compliance – Mind the Gap* is just such a text. Susan Groundwater-Smith and Nicole Mockler, both of them academic practitioners who remain close to school practice, have constructed a sophisticated series of interlocking chapters that manage to be simultaneously cautious and celebratory of the manifold ways in which teachers learn.

The book has been designed to specifically examine current trends towards practitioner inquiry as a keystone upon which teacher professional learning may be built, then develop and finally flourish. It argues for a more sophisticated and liberatory stance than one that sees inquiry into practice as a means of maintaining fidelity with the policies of employing authorities in many education jurisdictions in countries such as Australasia, the United Kingdom and North America. It suggests that the press for such compliance leaves little room for a more critical position to be adopted, but that if teachers are indeed to further learn, unlearn and relearn then they need to be alert to the ways in which the press to compliance effectively de-professionalizes them. In this respect this book challenges teachers to a certain type of disruptive practice, both in terms of how they operate in their classrooms but also how they examine and live their professional lives.

There exist many texts designed to enumerate the characteristics of effective professional learning for teachers, such as ensuring: that it is focused upon student learning needs; that it is enacted in environments that embed it in practice, that it allows for both pressure and support from government agencies; and, that it is based upon soundly assembled evidence. However, appealing and useful as these may be they do little to further a more critical discussion of the ways in which teachers may learn in a context of teacher agency and ethical practice.

The book is divided into four parts. The first of these examines the ways in which regimes of compliance have been established within existing professional cultures, especially those conducted by significant employers of teachers within state instrumentalities. It explores historical and future possibilities and enjoins the readers to take courage in the exercise of moral purpose and virtue. The second section examines the nature of professional knowledge itself and the ways in which the professional voice can be better represented in a discourse of quality. The third part of the book explores the tension, contradictions, dilemmas and challenges and raises some thorny questions in relation to accountability and the operation of communities of practice. The final part of the book moves to cases that allow for that which has come in preceding chapters to be woven into a coherent narrative of practice.

The book embodies conceptual and philosophical arguments but is strongly grounded in the world of practice itself. While the latter part contains case studies the earlier chapters draw extensively on the school-based work of the authors, both of whom have long been engaged in supporting and sustaining practitioner inquiry.

I believe that this book will be an important one for those concerned with professional learning in the field of education. It is particularly timely in our changing world where major economic and social changes are burgeoning. It begins with four problematics which, understood as current orthodoxies, might be seen to pose a threat to progressive education and authentic, generative professional learning, these being the rise of audit cultures, the standardisation of practice, the diminishment of teacher professional judgement and the 'quality' agenda in education.

It concludes by making hope practical with a call to action, for the teaching profession itself as well as those who serve it by continuing to pose a challenge to the compliance agenda in all of its manifestations. Not a challenge to be taken lightly, but one that is compelling, intrinsically rewarding and honourable.

Professor Judyth Sachs
Deputy Vice Chancellor and Provost
Macquarie University

Contents

Part III   Tensions, Contradictions, Competing Agendas

7   What Is at Stake and What Is at Risk 83

**8   Who Pays the Piper? Agendas, Priorities
and Accountabilities** 93

9   What Learning Community? A Knotty Problem 101

Part IV   Closing the Gap

Part I
Present, Past and Future

Chapter 1
Introduction: Current Problematics in Teacher Professional Learning

> *While it is desirable that all educational institutions should be
> equipped so as to give students an opportunity for acquiring
> and testing ideas and information in active pursuits typifying
> important social situations, it will, doubtless, be a long time
> before all of them are thus furnished.*
>
> (Dewey 1916: 132)

Almost a century after the publication of *Democracy and Education*, we find ourselves in uncertain and ambiguous times. Despite the efforts and indeed triumphs of individual teachers and schools, on a policy level we appear to be once again retreating from a once-within-our-grasp vision of progressive education into safer, more measurable and quantifiable territory. More worryingly, we see the very notion of democracy at the heart of Dewey's thinking under threat, not only at the hands of terrorists mounting militant attacks on 'the west', but perhaps more disturbingly at the hands of religious, economic and educational fundamentalists and a pervasive neoliberal educational agenda. The appearance of *Democracy and Education* at number four on the *Human Events* list of the ten most harmful books of the nineteenth and twentieth centuries[1] (outranked only by Marx and Engels' *The Communist Manifesto*, Hitler's *Mein Kampf* and Mao's *Little Red Book*) serves to demonstrate the threat that progressive ideas about education and its role in the creation of civil society pose to conservative pundits and the post-9/11 social order. Security – in relation to national borders, energy, food, resources and other dimensions – is the primary concern within the new world order, but what of our educational security, and who and where are its warriors?

This book emerges from this context, from our staunch belief in the transformative and liberatory capacities and responsibilities of education, from a strong concern for what we perceive to be the 'gap' between these and current regimes of audit and

---

[1] "Ten Most Harmful Books of the 19th and 20th Centuries'", *Human Events* 31 May 31, 2005. Cited in Apple, M.W. (2006). *Educating the 'Right' Way: Markets, Standards, God and Inequality.* New York: RoutledgeFalmer. (2nd Eedition).

S. Groundwater-Smith and N. Mockler, *Teacher Professional Learning
in an Age of Compliance*, DOI: 10.1007/978-1-4020-9417-0_1,
© Springer Science+Business Media B.V. 2009

'standards', and from a deep desire to reverse the trend whereby simple, 'common-sense' solutions are applied to problems and contexts which are highly complex and ambiguous. For it appears to us that over the past decade on a societal level, our tolerance for ambiguity has dropped in inverse proportion to the rise in fear and mistrust we have seen, and while brave and courageous global leadership might well have gone some way towards alleviating this trend, there also we have experienced a dearth. The key premise upon which this book is based is that generative and ongoing inquiry-based teacher professional learning holds enormous potential to contribute to a transformative educational agenda, through providing an ongoing catalyst for improved pedagogy and practice.

This introductory chapter seeks to explore what we see as some of the key current problematics in teacher professional learning, emanating from the social context in which we live and its implications for education. These problematics emerge from our own understanding and experience of the current context as teacher educators, and more specifically, in our work supporting teachers in their professional learning. We seek not merely to paint a dire picture of the educational landscape here, but rather to offer a considered critique of some of the orthodoxies of our time and offer hope in the form of an alternate vision of education and specifically teacher professional learning. We need to state at the outset that while we write from an Australian context, drawing examples also from the UK, Europe and the USA, we are mindful of the particular nuances of these contexts. Where comparisons and contrasts are made, we make them in an attempt to 'make sense' of the global context of education and not without an understanding that such generalisations are of themselves problematic. Having said that, we are mindful that although this is an anglophone text, many of our colleagues working in other parts of the worlds are currently facing similar conditions and challenges.

Schooling the Audit Society

The first of the problematics that we seek to elucidate is the rise and rise of audit cultures, especially in relation to the provision of social services such as education. Much has been written in the past decade about the rise of audit cultures and associated 'rituals of verification' (Power 1999; Strathern 2000) within Western societies. Michael Power's recent work (2004, 2007) has explored the links between audit cultures and the rise of risk management across social institutions of varying kinds, arguing that the 'phenomenal expansion of the risk industry reflects a number of different but convergent pressures for change in organisational practices for dealing with *uncertainty*' (2004: 12). Power contends that the adoption of the notion of risk as an 'organising concept' (2004: 13) in public and private sector management thinking, largely a response to demands of control, both internal and external, within regimes of audit and 'accountability', is both a response to uncertainty and ambiguity and a driving force in the diminishment of social trust in judgement. He writes:

> The risk management of everything reflects the efforts of organisational agents previously engaged in the collectivisation and pooling of social and economic risks, to offload and re-individualise their own personal risk. The result is a potentially catastrophic downward spiral in which expert judgement shrinks to an empty form of defendable compliance. In this way the risk management of everything poses major risks to a society in which the most pressing and most unpredictable problems cannot be solved without the effective marshalling of expert knowledge and judgement. (Power 2004: 42)

Similarly, Castells (1997) writes of the impact of the current climate of uncertainty, wrought largely by the growth of capitalism and globalisation in the latter part of the twentieth century, upon social life, and the associated growth in a variety of extremisms and fundamentalisms (among them religious and market) by way of response. Castells' work is a call on the one hand to resistance of the dominant (neoliberal) paradigm and on the other to the rebuilding of civil society through the construction of new 'identities' and new social movements.

It is not our intention here to detail or dwell upon these complex ideas, but rather to consider the implications of the current socio-political context for education, and more specifically, teacher professional learning. Neoliberal and neoconservative political agendas at work in the USA, UK and Australia hold significant implications for the way education is positioned, practised and 'measured' within these societies. In the USA, the reauthorisation of the Elementary and Secondary Education Act of 2001/2, commonly known as 'No Child Left Behind' (NCLB), and in the UK, the Children Act 2004, commonly known as 'Every Child Matters' (ECM), are each practical manifestations of this neoliberal agenda, as are the recent attempts on the part of the Australian federal government to 'consolidate' state-based school curriculum, testing and reporting into a single national system. As Garrett has argued (2007), in parallel with the symbiotic relationship between the USA and the UK in terms of foreign policy (and here we extrapolate to include Australia) in the early twenty-first century a corresponding symbiosis has grown in relation to aspects of domestic policy, including approaches to education and children's services.

While ECM is far broader in its scope than NCLB, relating only in part to school education and providing a pathway for the integration of all aspects of childrens' services in the UK, it grows out of the same audit ideology that has governed the Ofsted system of inspection and ranking of schools since 1999 and is embedded in New Labour's approach to education. Further, the appropriation of progressive language within policies which seek to measure, codify and quantify educational outcomes in unhelpful ways and provide rationales for standardised testing regimes (Apple 2006: 90) provides a facade of care and concern laid over neoconservative approaches, which offer neither to those who are most vulnerable at the hands of these policies. Their truistic common-usage names are in themselves representative of the highly politicised context out of which each one emerged – very few educators would wish to argue that every child does not matter or that any child should be left behind and the 'soundbyte' culture of which they are an integral part.

In recent years, writers such as Sachs (2003b) and Apple (2000, 2006) have drawn upon the mainstream sociological literature as well as the rich heritage of radical and progressive education represented in the work of, for example, John Dewey and Paolo Freire, to argue for the adoption of a stance on the part of teachers and teacher educators which seeks to interrupt the dominant neoliberal, neoconservative and managerial discourses surrounding education through the seizing of what Sachs has called an 'activist identity' (2003). Sachs (2001: 14–15) summarises activist professionalism as that which is:

- Based on democratic principles
- Negotiated
- Collaborative
- Socially critical
- Future oriented
- Strategic and tactical

The ideals of the activist teaching profession, however, stand in direct opposition to the ideals of what teachers should be and should do as representatives and enforcers of the audit society; furthermore, the more fully entrenched neoliberal and neoconservative agendas become in educational and social discourses, the more difficult it becomes, on both individual and collective levels, for teachers to respond to this call.

Standards and Standardisation: The One Size Fits All Agenda

As a principal tool of the audit society, professional standards for teachers have become a global phenomenon in Western societies in recent years. A physical manifestation of the managerial discourses which have infiltrated education in the past decade, standards are sometimes regarded as a panacea for an ailing teaching profession and/or education system, and to have the capacity to raise the profile of the profession, improve teachers' performance and facilitate more effective professional development for teachers (Sachs 2003a). While we do not wish to suggest that professional standards cannot play a part in the achievement of higher status of the profession and play a useful part in teacher professional learning, we believe neither that professional standards will alone be successful in doing either, nor that either would be impossible without the existence of standards. Linda Darling-Hammond's warning about the possible 'pifalls' of standards for the teaching profession is salient here:

> Teaching standards are not a magic bullet. By themselves, they cannot solve the problems of dysfunctional school organizations, outmoded curricula, inequitable allocation of resources, or lack of social supports for children and youth. Standards, like all reforms, hold their own dangers. Standard setting in all professions must be vigilant against the possibilities that practice could become constrained by the codification of knowledge that does not significantly acknowledge legitimate diversity of approaches or advances in the field; that access to practice could become overly restricted on grounds not directly related to competence; or that adequate learning opportunities for candidates to meet standards may not emerge on an equitable basis. (Darling-Hammond 1999: 39)

A brief scan of the current iterations of teaching standards around the world reveals that in the UK, and more specifically in England, professional teaching standards are administered by the Training and Development Agency for Schools (TDA), and 'underpinned by the five key outcomes for children and young people identified in Every Child Matters'.[2] Released in June 2007 for implementation in the new academic year, the standards are linked to pay scales for teachers in England, and encompass description of professional proficiency at five levels, from 'qualified teacher status' (i.e. graduate) to the 'advanced skills teacher'. Engaging with the standards is mandatory for new teachers and those wishing to 'advance' their regard and pay scale.

In the USA, national professional teaching standards are overseen by the National Board for Professional Teaching Standards (NBPTS), which provides certification for teachers on a voluntary basis. According to recent projections, approximately 2% of the nation's teachers will have acquired national board certification by 2008. Mandatory certification and registration is overseen by state bodies, with each state providing registration for teachers according to state-developed professional standards. In addition, the No Child Left Behind legislation mandated that from the end of the 2005/6 academic year all teachers be certified as 'Highly Qualified' using what is known as the 'High Objective Uniform State Evaluation' (HOUSE) process. According to the NCLB act, highly qualified teachers are those who:

- Hold a bachelor's degree
- Hold full state certification or licensure
- Prove that they know each subject they teach (USDOE 2004: 2)

'Proof' that teachers 'know' the subject/s that they are teaching can be provided via a range of methods under the HOUSE process, including evidence that teachers have completed university study at either undergraduate or postgraduate level in the field, and participation in continuing professional development activities. Furthermore, certification as a highly qualified teacher under the act, given that it entails full certification at state level, necessarily involves the meeting of professional standards in the teacher's home state.

In the Australian context also, there is a proliferation of professional teaching standards developed by state accreditation boards such as the NSW Institute of Teachers, professional subject associations, and more recently a process has been initiated by Teaching Australia, the Australian Institute for Teaching and School Leadership to develop standards for advanced teaching and school leadership. In the current context, teachers are required to be accredited by the relevant state-based body at a basic level of professional competence, with additional accreditation optional at a higher level. The development of national standards was part of an initiative on the part of previous federal government to introduce performance-based pay for outstanding teachers, one of several current measures designed to

---

[2] TDA News Release 22 June 2007, *TDA Launch Professional Standards for Teachers*, available at http://www.tda.gov.uk/about/mediarelations/2007/20070622.aspx. Accessed 14 August 2007.

wrest control of education back from state governments, and a measure which within the rhetoric presented by the federal government should improve the attraction and retention of the 'best and brightest' into teaching. How far this policy agenda will be pursued by the newly elected Labour government is still unclear, although initial indications suggest that the general direction will be pursued, albeit utilising slightly more progressive strategies and approaches.

Professional standards and the expectation that they will somehow provide a cure for an ailing teaching profession are common to each of these three national contexts. Further, many similarities can be discerned between the professional standards themselves, despite the painstaking local consultation and joint construction processes that the various accreditation bodies have engaged in the processes of their development. While we agree with Darling-Hammond when she suggests that standards hold the potential for 'opening up' critical professional discourse, 'enhancing the establishment of shared norms by making teaching public and collegial' (Darling-Hammond 1999: 39), it is our fear that the current standards regimes and the policy contexts out of which they grow have at their hearts a desire not to build an understanding of the complexity and nuance of teaching practice or to celebrate the diversity of teachers and learners, but rather to standardise practice, stifle debate and promote the fallacious notion of 'professional objectivity'.

Subjectivity in the Classroom: The Vanishing of Teacher Professional Judgement

The loss of appeal to teacher professional judgement is problematic in terms of continuing professional learning. In an educational context, we understand teacher professional judgement to be a key and critical element of professional practice: the capacity to make wise and sound decisions about learning based upon knowledge of learning itself, knowledge of the student and knowledge of the learning context is core to the carriage of good teaching and learning. Further, we are committed to the notion, advanced by Lawrence Stenhouse, that the development and use of teacher professional judgement is inextricably linked to the emancipatory or trans-formative dimensions of education. Stenhouse wrote:

> The essence of emancipation, as I conceive it, is the intellectual, moral and spiritual autonomy which we recognise when we eschew paternalism and the rule of authority and hold ourselves obliged to appeal to judgement. Emancipation rests not merely on the right of a person to exercise intellectual, moral and spiritual judgement, but upon the passionate belief that the virtue of humanity is diminished … when judgement is overruled by authority. (Stenhouse 1979a: 163)

In the passage from his work quoted above, Michael Power writes of the impact of regimes of risk management on the development and carriage of expert judgement, casting it as a 'potentially catastrophic downward spiral in which expert judgement shrinks to an empty form of defendable compliance' (Power 2004: 42).

We see that the diminishment of teacher professional judgement has taken place in incremental steps over the past 2 decades, in inverse proportion to the rise in popularity of standardised testing, 'objective' assessment and the codification and quantification of teachers' knowledge and practice via professional standards. The prevailing 'common-sense' approach to education holds at its centre the equation of objective measures with 'accountability' and the 'fuzzy' measures represented in the application of teacher professional judgement with the much less desirable and indeed indefensible 'subjectivity'. This dichotomy, long utilised within the neoconservative drive for standardised testing is neither helpful nor in fact accurate, for in advocating the advancement and development of teacher professional judgement, we do so in the understanding that finely honed professional judgement is a tool by which teachers can be held more, not less, accountable, albeit to the right 'masters' to their students, their colleagues and their communities for the quality and improvement of student learning.

Quality: A Catch Cry for Our Time

Also emanating from global managerial discourses, what Clarke and Newman refer to as the 'epidemic of quality' (Clarke and Newman 1997: 76) has taken hold in the educational context in parallel with its ascendancy in public sector management. Like motherhood, it is difficult to be opposed to quality. It is less difficult, however, to be opposed to mindless adherence to ideals and virtues elevated within the corporate sector, where there exists a simplicity of purpose and process, which does not figure in the context of education and the complex business that is teaching and learning.

While we do not deny that the issue of quality is of enormous importance within the educational enterprise, here we wish to pose the question 'quality for whom?', and to suggest that there exists a large and important distinction between the aims and processes of quality assurance and quality control. While we see that in an educational context the notion of quality control relates to the development of processes that aim to ensure equity of access to 'quality' teaching and learning and that which Marzano refers to as 'the guaranteed and viable curriculum' (2003), processes of quality assurance are generally focused upon the gathering of evidence to build confidence in the quality of educational services provided. That is to say that it is quite possible for quality assurance processes to deal with the construction of the *perception* of quality rather than the provision of actual quality itself. We wish to flag here that on a global level, where increasingly in western societies we are focused on the building of confidence in educational institutions and processes, represented, for example, in the requirement of the No Child Left Behind Act that states ensure that 100% of teachers are 'Highly Qualified', the processes whereby such confidence is built are often thin themselves when it comes to 'quality'. The endless tick-boxes and 'administrivia' associated with quality assurance provide a wealth of 'evidence', which in turn reportedly has the capacity to build public confidence (as well as contribute to the intensification of teachers' work), but we posit that the real issue of quality lies well beyond the public relations exercise of quality assurance, in the core business of teaching and learning and providing care and support for young people. There is no 'quick fix' in the provision of quality in these quarters – rather, quality teaching and learning is underwritten by sound teacher professional judgement, critical professional discourse between colleagues and access to professional development and learning, which is engaging, situated and relevant to teachers' needs and those of their students.

These, then, are for us, the key problematics impacting upon teacher professional learning in the current context. This book aims to provide a response to these in the form of a rationale for inquiry-based teacher professional learning, which we believe to be more critical than ever in current, problematic times. While the culture of compliance represented in the problematics discussed above increasingly draws us to an approach to teacher professional learning that is 'training' oriented, quantifiable and easily measured or 'ticked off' for quality assurance purposes, we will argue throughout this book that for teacher professional learning to serve the burgeoning needs of students and their teachers in the twenty-first century, we must value and vigorously pursue an alternative model.

Our Framework and the Book's Structure

It is our contention that these problematics are representative of the compliance agenda's impact upon teacher professional learning and education more broadly. It is hoped that this book might provide something of a 'circuit breaker', in returning to the underpinnings and historical foundations of inquiry-based professional learning and posing a challenge to some of the orthodoxies of our time. While we do not wish to promote inquiry-based professional learning as a universal remedy, we hope that in 'taking stock' of where we are, raising some difficult questions about doctrines which are often taken for granted and their potential for harm, and pointing to possible directions for the future which are both generative and practical, we might offer a vision for the future that is both courageous and hope-filled.

The book is thus divided into four parts. In Part I, *Present, Past and Future*, we aim to provide a 'snapshot' of the context of inquiry-based teacher professional learning. Chapter 2 includes a historical survey of traditions of teacher inquiry, practitioner inquiry and action research as they evolved over the course of the twentieth century and into the early twenty-first century, with particular emphasis upon the growth of practitioner inquiry within a critical tradition. We contrast this with what we see as the appropriation of practitioner inquiry by the state in recent years as an implementation tool, and draw on examples from both the UK and Australia to illustrate the challenges this presents to the emancipatory and critical dimensions of these traditions. In Chapter 3, we offer a new vision for teacher inquiry, exploring the links between what Fullan has termed 'moral purpose' (Fullan 1993, 2001) and the development of professional courage. We argue for inquiry-based professional learning as a tool for developing a courageous and risk-taking orientation to education, drawing upon examples of teachers and schools involved in largely unfunded investigations centred on real and important concerns for their students and school communities.

In Part II, *Professional Knowledge Building: Tenets and Tools*, we reflect on the nature and creation of teacher professional knowledge, arguing for inquiry as a framework for professional learning, which functions as a catalyst for both the development and the dissemination of professional knowledge. In Chapter 4, we develop the notion of 'Mode 3 Knowledge', suggesting a 'third way' to understand professional knowledge which both informs the profession and the academic study of the field. In Chapter 5, we expand the notion of inquiry as a framework for teacher professional learning, drawing on Cochran-Smith and Lytle's notion of 'inquiry as stance' (Cochran-Smith and Lytle 2007) to suggest that inquiry-based professional learning provides an effective and powerful way to disrupt some of the dominant discourses and problematics currently at work in education. Chapter 6 constitutes a call for the reclaiming of 'quality' as a key element and tool of teacher professional knowledge, arguing for the development of new dimensions of quality opposed to the 'emperor's new clothes' approach of 'quality assurance'.

Part III, *Tensions, Contradictions, Competing Agendas*, explores some of the current directions in inquiry-based teacher professional learning. In Chapter 7, we explore the elements 'at stake' and 'at risk' in inquiry-based work for teachers across school and higher education sectors, arguing for the integration of student voice with those of other stakeholders and exploring the 'risky business' dimension of asking pertinent (and perhaps sometimes *im*pertinent) questions. Chapter 8 focuses on the multiple agendas, priorities and accountabilities of those engaged in practitioner inquiry and explores some of the constraints and compromises present when agendas and priorities are established outside of the school or community context. In Chapter 9, we explore the 'easy to say, hard to do' concept of the learning community as a framework or home for inquiry-based professional learning, drawing on a range of examples from different continents and contexts.

Finally, in Part IV, *Closing the Gap*, we offer two case studies of inquiry-based professional learning, both individual and systemic, drawn from both school and higher education contexts, which challenge current orthodoxies and respond to the critical and emancipatory dimension of practitioner inquiry. We argue that, while it is neither desirable nor possible for these models to be 'transplanted' into differing contexts, salient learnings are embedded in each which have implications for educators and educational communities more broadly.

Conclusion: Inquiry-Based Teacher Professional Learning in an Age of Compliance

In conclusion, it is our hope that this book will constitute a call to the teaching profession and teacher educators to recognise the difference between 'being good' and 'doing good'. In the current age of compliance, rarely do they overlap.

For 'being good' within the audit society is demonstrated by compliance with the orthodoxies of our day, a willingness to adopt and interact with the discourses and problematics outlined earlier in this chapter. 'Doing good', however, is another matter. Putting the needs of young people and indeed the transformational dimensions of education at the heart of professional practice requires courage and willingness on the part of educators to be deeply countercultural, and it is our hope that this book will provide a challenge to the profession to do just that.

Chapter 2
How Did We Get Here? Historical Perspectives on Inquiry-Based Professional Learning

> *I believe that some - perhaps most - action research no longer aspires to having this critical edge, especially in the bigger sense of social or educational critique aimed at transformation of the way things are. Much of the action research that has proliferated in many parts of the world over the past two decades has not been the vehicle for educational critique we hoped it would be. Instead, some may even have become a vehicle for domesticating students and teachers to conventional forms of schooling.*
>
> (Kemmis 2006: 459)

Despite its recent rise to popularity, inquiry-based teacher professional learning has a long history, forged out of traditions in the UK, the USA and Australia. In this chapter, we draw on these traditions to give an overview of the historical 'roots' of inquiry-based professional learning, exploring 'action research', 'teacher research' and 'practitioner inquiry' in particular, and arguing, along with Kemmis, that while we strongly advocate for this kind of teacher professional learning as a vehicle to 'transformation of the way things are', recent experience has shown that 'more' is not necessarily 'better'.

Inquiry-based professional learning puts action research or teacher inquiry to work in the name of teacher professional learning. At its best it is:

• Focused upon transformation, of both self and school
• Collaborative, with opportunities for teachers to build authentic collegiality
• Ongoing, rather than solely project-based
• Capable of engaging teachers in creating knowledge about and for practice
• Encompassing of opportunities for teachers to develop and hone their professional judgement

In developing this understanding of the potential of inquiry-based teacher professional learning, we have drawn upon a rich and complex scholarly tradition, and it is our intention in this chapter to locate our ideas within this historical context and tradition.

The chapter is presented in three sections. In the first, we examine some of the key scholarships in order to highlight the field's depth and diversity in historical

S. Groundwater-Smith and N. Mockler, *Teacher Professional Learning in an Age of Compliance*, DOI: 10.1007/978-1-4020-9417-0_2,
© Springer Science + Business Media B.V. 2009

terms. In the second, we explore notions of 'academic legitimacy' and knowledge creation as they are represented in the arena of teacher research. In the final section, we look at recent trends towards the appropriation of inquiry-based professional learning as an implementation tool.

Inquiry-Based Professional Learning: Historical 'Roots' and Traditions

The idea that teachers can and should undertake research is closely linked to ideas about knowledge creation, as well as to primary beliefs about the role and nature of teaching and education. This section aims to situate contemporary paradigms of teacher research and inquiry-based professional learning within a historical framework dating back to the beginning of the last century, to evaluate and critique those contemporary paradigms in the context of current discourses around education and knowledge and to define and discuss salient issues arising from the research.

In terms of scale, while we take a historical view of the development of notions of teacher research, the majority of the key texts discussed here belong to the 'second wave' of the teacher research movement, heralded by the publication of works such as Carr and Kemmis' *Becoming Critical: Education, Knowledge and Action Research* (1986) and Goswami and Stilman's *Reclaiming the Classroom: Teacher Research as an Agency for Change* (1987) or later.

Perspectives on teacher research are diverse, ranging from those where teacher research is not equated with research at all (Huberman 1996), to radical notions of teacher research as a new and independent model of research and an emerging discourse in its entirety (Berthoff 1987; Cochran-Smith and Lytle 1993). Teacher research is often construed as a means to the achievement of other goals or objectives for teachers and schools: effective teacher professional development, the enhancement of teacher professionalism, curriculum development and innovation, systemic and organisational change and the enhanced democratisation of education and society more broadly have all been seen as the possible products of teacher research over time.

Definitions and Categorisations

Teacher research is a diverse field. For our purposes, notions of action research, practitioner research, teacher inquiry and collaborative research will be treated together under the banner of 'practitioner inquiry'. Each of these, along with the more ephemeral 'action learning' (which we shall discuss in the final section of this chapter) are examples of inquiry-based professional learning. This is not to deny or ignore the differences between different 'branches', but rather to place the focus of this discussion onto broader issues of purpose and epistemology, as well as the significant issues which emerge from various paradigms. On this issue, Marion Dadds and Susan Hart write:

> While there may be characteristic differences in these several research methodologies (i.e. practitioner, action and teacher research), they share in common a central commitment to the study of one's own professional practice by the researcher himself or herself, with a view to improving that practice for the benefit of others. (2001: 7)

While we agree with their assessment, some clarifications follow in the charting of the historical development of practitioner inquiry. It is worth noting that while it is possible to make broad distinctions between 'branches', such distinctions are often arbitrary in practice.

Action Research: A Tactic for Social Change

The roots of 'action research' are situated broadly within the field of social reform in the work of John Collier and Kurt Lewin and within the field of education in the work of John Dewey and Stephen Corey (Noffke 1997). In the school context, action research seeks to give teachers practical methods through which to reflect on and document their experience, leading to tangible classroom improvement. Implicit in the notion of 'action research' is a practical critical framework which assists practitioners in undertaking systematic enquiry into their own practice, as well as a mechanism for building and testing theory within their own work.

In his work at the beginning of the twentieth century, John Dewey called for teachers to become students of learning, both consumers and creators of knowledge about teaching and learning. He saw teachers who were 'adequately moved by their own ideas and intelligence' (Dewey 1904: 16) as the remedy for faddism in education, integrating elements of what has subsequently become known as 'reflective practice' (Schon 1983). This notion of teacher as knowledge creator is one which has been greatly debated in literature on teacher research in recent years, and one to which we shall return at a later point in this chapter.

Dewey's focus on the active participation of teachers in research was further developed in the work of Stephen Corey on educational action research (1953). Much of Corey's work focuses upon the establishment of action research in education as a 'legitimate' form of educational research. His work can be seen as complementary to that of Dewey in that Dewey's notion of teacher as active participant coupled with Corey's assertion of a new form of research represent a new vision of the teaching profession, 'which has, at its core, a valuing of teachers' knowledge and work (Noffke 1997: 316).

In her historical account of the development of action research within the North American context, Susan Noffke draws attention to the seminal role of John Collier, US Commissioner of Indian Affairs in the 1930s, who established policies and practices consistent with goals of self-regulation and self-sufficiency for those whom he served. His 'focus on grass roots interests, on collaboration ... and on the need for direct links to social action for improvement' (Noffke : 312) planted the seeds for the development of action research for social change (Noffke 1997a, b), as picked up and extended by Kurt Lewin in the 1940s.

Lewin defined action research as 'comparative research on the conditions and effects of various forms of social action, and research leading to social action' (Lewin 1946: 202–203). For Lewin, in order for the research findings to be truly actionable, the processes and practices must necessarily be situated within the discourses of those being researched. He writes: '[S]ocially, it does not suffice that university organisations produce new scientific insight … it will be necessary to install fact-finding procedures, social eyes and ears right into social action bodies' (p.206). In the work of Lewin we see the origins of the processes and techniques of action research applied generally to the improvement of society, informed perhaps by his own experiences as a post-war refugee. As Noffke (1997) observes Lewin's and Collier's work share a focus on the necessarily collaborative and cyclical nature of action research as a vehicle for social change, as well as the process of studying theoretical and practical problems together. It is upon these notions as well as those reflected in the work of Dewey and Corey that the field of action research in education has developed throughout the course of the latter half of the twentieth century, in a variety of international contexts, and it is to these that we now turn.

Teacher Inquiry: The UK Experience

The roots of the teacher inquiry movement in the UK can be found in the work of Lawrence Stenhouse in the Humanities Curriculum Project (HCP). Teacher research developed as a tool for curriculum development in addressing the institutionalisation of social inequalities in the education system through the reform of humanities education in the 1960s and 1970s (Elliott 1997). While action research is often the preferred approach of teacher inquiry (Sachs 1999), the notion of teacher inquiry is essentially about teachers gathering and using evidence to improve classroom practice and enhance their understanding of their own knowledge and expertise. Sharing their understanding with others, both within and beyond their immediate environment is a critical part of this process for Stenhouse.

In his application of Lewin's notion of action research to the education setting, Stenhouse argued that teacher research is defined as that where the research act (which aims at finding something out) is also necessarily the substantive act (which aims at improving learning). Teacher research, he claimed, should also aim to make a contribution to the theory of education which is accessible to other teachers and enters into the critical discourse of the profession (Stenhouse 1985c). In this way, Stenhouse developed the notion of research as 'systematic enquiry made public' (Stenhouse 1980: 1), advocating to teacher researchers as well as academic researchers the need to publish more to the 'village' within which the research is conducted and less 'to the world' (Stenhouse 1981: 17). Throughout his work, Stenhouse attacked paradigms of research which place teacher research below academic research in a hierarchy of legitimacy, arguing for the acceptance of teacher-as-researcher by the academic community as a legitimate form of field-based research (Stenhouse 1985b) and advocating for the application of the illuminative research tradition within classrooms as a means to utilising and strengthening professional judgement (Stenhouse 1979b, 1985a).

Stenhouse and his colleagues developed a paradigm of action research which aimed to 'demystify and democratise research' (Rudduck and Hopkins 1985), as a response to their perception that educational research was not contributing effectively to the improvement of classroom practice and the building of a reflective and reflexive capacity in teachers. Throughout his work, Stenhouse consistently argued for the acknowledgement of the limitations of psycho-statistical research methods within the field of education (Stenhouse 1985b) and the acceptance of the teacher researcher as 'presumably a better tester of theory than the professional researcher', contending that 'perhaps it is difficult for the [academic] researcher to admit practitioner research because it means a diminution of his [sic.] power vis-à-vis teachers' (Stenhouse 1985a: 132).

Stenhouse's definition of research and philosophy of teacher-as-researcher has been instrumental in the development of contemporary paradigms of teacher research. His ideas have informed the work of scholars in this area, evident not only in British scholarship but also much of that which has emanated from Australia. while Noffke (1997b) construes the work of Stenhouse as a move away from research for the purpose of social change and towards research as professional development and personal change on the part of individual teachers, the framework of critical social change within which the HCP and the subsequent work of Stenhouse and CARE was situated would seem to counter this argument, highlighting that this UK branch of teacher research centred simultaneously on social change *and* teacher professional development.

It is important to note here the participatory and collaborative nature of the research advocated by Stenhouse and his colleagues. The research process itself is seen to be a collaborative venture, aimed at strengthening community and understanding through inquiry. This notion of the participatory and collaborative nature of teacher research is further evident in the work of Bridget Somekh who, in advocating for teachers and academics to step into each others' shoes in the interests of collaboration and mutual understanding (Somekh 1994), argues for the need to bridge the 'discourse gap' between the school and the academy through the negotiation and sharing of power between each partner engaged in the research process. In recognising that

> we live in a world of action, a world in which the nature of existence is shaped by perceptions, and this strongly suggests that knowledge constructed without the active participation of practitioners can only be partial knowledge. (1994: 367)

Somekh reiterates and progresses the arguments of Stenhouse and Elliott, after Collier and Lewin, that active participation of the practitioner is a necessary element in the construction of new knowledge for the profession.

Over the past decade, these ideas have been extended by UK scholars into the area of pupil or student voice. The works of Jean Rudduck (e.g. Rudduck and

Flutter 2006; Rudduck 2006) and Michael Fielding (e.g. 2004a, 2007) have been particularly influential in establishing a rationale for practitioners researching alongside young people, building collaboration and opening up opportunities for agency in new directions. We shall take this issue up at greater length in Chapter 7 and again in the case studies presented in Chapter 11.

Practitioner Research and Collaborative Inquiry: The Australian Experience

Australian approaches to teacher as researcher build on notions of collaboration and participation developed by Stenhouse and his colleagues in the UK, with emphasis on the critical and political possibilities of teacher inquiry (Kemmis and Grundy 1997).

In their seminal work, Wilfred Carr and Stephen Kemmis (1986) argue for the emancipatory power of action research for teachers, linking the social research dimension of action research to social action through the critical connection with educational (and thus social) improvement. In a subsequent work, Kemmis writes:

> [Emancipatory or critical action research] is always critical, in the sense that it is about relentlessly trying to understand and improve the way things are in relation to how they could be better. (Kemmis 1993: 3)

For Carr and Kemmis, the purpose of teacher research is to mount a radical challenge to the status quo, particularly those aspects of the system which permit, reinforce and perpetuate systemic inequities. Kemmis argues for the need for academic researchers to forge links with practitioner researchers, employing Habermas' (1987) theory of communicative action as his epistemological rationale for this argument.

In a subsequent work, Kemmis further employs the work of Habermas to highlight the need for university-based researchers and practitioner researchers to enter communicative space together in a relationship of reciprocity and in emancipatory and critical interests, claiming that 'communicative action is at the heart of education - at the heart of the educational process itself' (Kemmis 2001: 13), and further that 'education consists in learning and practicing the arts of communicative action', that is, the opening up of dialogue and debate around the form, function and processes of education by those practising and researching its fabric. This argument further extends that of Somekh, discussed above.

These notions are extended in a practical direction by Shirley Grundy, who conceptualises practitioner research as a means for teacher professional development and ultimately, school improvement, contending that action research is necessarily a collaborative enterprise, which may or may not involve an external or academic 'significant other' (1995: 6). Her conclusions suggest that her underlying epistemology is one which sees teachers as active creators of professional knowledge for and about teaching. Her earlier typology of action research modes (Grundy 1982), which draws a distinction between technical, practical and emancipatory models

of action research and argues for the development of action research which eman-
cipates teachers from 'the dictates of compulsions of tradition, precedent, habit,
coercion as well as from self-deception' (1982: 358) would also indicate this.

Australian articulations of teacher research often integrate elements of collaborative
inquiry, which draws school-based and university-based researchers into partnership
for the purpose of conducting research which is mutually beneficial and cross-
contextual. Collaborative inquiry has often been conducted as part of large funded
projects such as Innovative Links (Sachs 1997) or those associated with the
National Schools Network (Groundwater-Smith 1998), and requires of participants
high levels of communication and intercultural awareness (Sachs 1999). This
emphasis on collaboration and partnership reflects once again the strong links
between the UK and Australian versions of teacher research.

Teacher Research: The US Experience

The roots of the teacher research movement which has emerged in the USA over
the past 20 years can also be traced back to the origins of action research in the
work of Dewey and Lewin (Noffke 1997). The working definition of teacher
research provided by Marilyn Cochran-Smith and Susan Lytle as 'systematic
and intentional inquiry carried out by teachers' (1993: 7) owes an acknowledged
debt to Stenhouse's notion, discussed above, of research as systematic inquiry
made public.

Teacher research in the USA has emerged as a challenge to dominant paradigms
of teacher education, pedagogy and the social order itself, finding its roots also in
the feminist, civil rights and other critical social movements of the last quarter of
the twentieth century. While the methodological contribution of Stenhouse and his
colleagues to the teacher research movement is often cited by American scholars
(see, e.g. Hollingsworth 1994), the challenge to the status quo mounted by teacher
researchers and their movement is often presented by American scholars as unique
to the American articulation of teacher as researcher (see Noffke 1997b). This tends
to ignore the origins of teacher inquiry in the UK, where, as argued above, notions
of teacher as researcher grew out of radical challenge to the dominant social order,
reinforced as it was seen, through the education system. As such, the parallels
between the UK and the USA versions of teacher as researcher can be seen to be
more numerous than generally acknowledged in the American literature.

Noffke (1994) surveys the historical landscape of teacher research in order to
identify the multiple purposes to which it is applied. She argues that 'action
research' is employed for a variety of purposes throughout the western world, ranging broadly from the education of teachers in conducting and applying research in
their work to challenging and arresting the systemic status quo. Noffke clearly sees
teacher research as located within a discourse of social reform, calling for scholars
to address what is for her a key issue: 'Placing action research into existing frames
for epistemology may also lead to new ways of maintaining privilege systems as

they are' (1994: 16). She continues on to suggest that the work of feminist and post-colonial scholars might provide some clues as to how best to break the tyranny of 'old' hierarchical or patriarchal epistemologies. Her argument here is essentially that the teacher research movement can be seen to parallel the women's movement in terms of the creation of alternate forms of scholarly discourse which reach different levels of acceptance within the academy, a claim further developed by Sandra Hollingsworth (1997).

In practice, the American version of teacher research seeks to place the control and direction of teacher inquiry into the hands of teachers themselves, where the research process and practice can be an intensely personal and individual enterprise, an approach which does differ from the UK and Australian versions with their emphasis on participatory and collaborative workings, and which perhaps reflects an epistemology grown out of links with social rather than necessarily educational reform. Also reflecting this origin is the contemporary emphasis in the USA, named by Hollingsworth and Sockett (1994) as 'how schools and teaching are shaped and institutionalised in society, what knowledge is privileged and what epistemological views are important for their transformation' (p.9). This focus is reflected in Schon's (1983) development of the notion of an epistemology of practice, in the application of such notions to ideas about teacher professionalism and professional identity (Sockett 1993), and in the work of scholars such as Cochran-Smith and Lytle, in their claim that 'research by teachers represents a distinctive way of knowing about teaching and learning that will alter - not just add to - what we know in the field' (1993: 325).

Contested Ground: Academic 'Legitimacy' and Knowledge Creation

Practitioner Research and 'The Academy'

Teacher research is political insofar as it challenges epistemologies which locate power and knowledge within traditional structures of the academy, giving voice to teachers and providing teachers with a way of interpreting, documenting and sharing their own knowledge. We believe that dichotomies which set teacher research against academic research and equate difference as inequality are neither helpful nor generative, although they still underpin much of the discussion around the legitimacy of practitioner research. The perspective on practitioner research expressed by Michael Huberman contrasts with that of Judyth Sachs and Ivor Goodson to provide an illustration of the way this argument typically plays out.

Huberman's 1996 article entitled "Moving Mainstream: Taking a Closer Look at Teacher Research" is an almost angry critique of models of teacher as researcher in which Huberman manages to raise as many questions about the inconsistency of his own epistemological framework as he does issues relating to teacher research. He begins by situating his argument historically within the discourse of practitioner research through references to Kurt Lewin, Lawrence Stenhouse and John Elliott, using their work as the basis to speculate 'I wonder how many US teacher researchers know that theirs is far from an original movement?' (Huberman 1996). He essentially argues that the teacher-research movement is engaged in activity which is (a) nothing new, (b) spurious in its nature due to the inability of researchers to accurately 'measure' and document their own experience, and (c) not a legitimate form of research as defined by the academy. Harsh judgement indeed from one who defines himself as a 'critical friend' (p.124) to teacher researchers. Despite his claims to the contrary, nestled within his discussion of philosophers from Giambattista Vico to Claude Levi-Strauss, Huberman is epistemologically positioned (trapped, one might argue) within a paradigm which sees him tied to the very dichotomies challenged by the philosophies that underpin practitioner inquiry.

Huberman does, however, raise some interesting and important issues related to teacher research and knowledge. In arguing that by virtue of their status as 'insiders', teachers are doomed in their research efforts to produce introspective accounts abundant with 'preconceptions, distortions and self-delusions' (p.128), Huberman raises questions around the 'inside' perspective in teacher research, casting as a negative what many have conceptualised as a positive. On this issue, Marilyn Cochran-Smith and Susan Lytle write:

> The debate here is not, as Huberman seems to suggest, one of generalisability and truth, on the one hand, versus context-specific and biased information on the other. Rather, the debate is related to larger questions about the kinds, forms and perspectives on knowledge that will ultimately help to improve educational practice. (Cochran-Smith and Lytle 1998: 26)

In his defence of the supremacy of the university-based researcher, grounded in his reading of Aristotle's much misunderstood distinction between *episteme* ('owned', in Huberman's view, by the academy) and *techne* (the province of the practitioner), Huberman raises another important issue, namely that of the gap between academic and teacher researchers and the boundaries that divide them. Finally, and related to the first issue, Huberman raises the question of teacher and school as knowledge creator and related issues of professional activism and professional knowledge.

In her 1997 work on the Innovative Links Between Schools and Universities Project for Teacher Professional Development (Sachs 1997), Judyth Sachs contends that teacher research, which occurs at a system-wide level, such as that involved in the Innovative Links project (see Yeatman and Sachs 1995), holds the potential to renew teacher professionalism, which, she argues, by its nature cannot be renewed at an individual or school level. She foregrounds her later work by arguing the need for educators to resist the urge to group academic research and practitioner research together as 'research', contending that when we do, 'we are not able to enquire into this relationship of mutual enrichment, what it looks like and how it should work' (p.456), or, to return to Habermas, it leaves us unable to open up the communicative space inherent in the relationship between the two.

Sachs further highlights issues around ownership of teacher research and differences between teacher and academic cultures in her work on teacher research and the strengthening and renewal of teacher professionalism. She draws upon her personal involvement in the Innovative Links Project and the Australian National Schools Network to address the questions 'how do you overcome the cultural differences between school-based practitioners and academics to facilitate a climate of professional reciprocity and secondly, whose research questions are investigated?' (1999: 41). Sachs construes the role of teachers and academics as different but reciprocal within the territory of school-based research, stressing the mutual benefits of collaborative inquiry for all involved as well as the need for both sides to acknowledge and be unapologetic for the difference in teacher and academic cultures. She argues that while collaborating with university-based researchers in school-based research has long been recognised as a significant professional development tool for teachers, it should also be recognised as a significant form of professional development for academics. In relation to the differences between teacher and academic cultures, she argues that 'it is the exigencies of classroom life that reinforces a pragmatic view rather than an anti-intellectual stance on the part of teachers' (1999: 47) that emphasises the differences and makes some boundaries very difficult to cross. In relation to the question of ownership, Sachs recognises the importance of the questions being posed collaboratively by practitioner and academic researchers, as well as considerable negotiation by all parties as to the nature of the research being undertaken and the forum within which it will be published. We have discussed the navigation of these issues within the context of professional learning at length elsewhere (Mockler and Groundwater-Smith 2009, forthcoming).

In her more recent work on the *activist professional*, Sachs (2000, 2003) further develops these concepts, arguing that the notion of the activist professional itself is founded upon, among other things, shared inquiry into practice, and that engaging in such activity 'provides a way for teachers to come to know the epistemological bases of their practice' (2003: 89–90). Furthermore, she contends that the projects which require practitioner and academic partners to collaborate assist in the development of a common language and framework for reflecting on and investigating classroom practice, creating spaces for 'new kinds of conversations to emerge' (2003: 92) which enrich debate around the improvement of practice. Sachs argues for the reinvention not only of teacher and school culture along the lines of professional activism, but also of teacher educators and the culture of their work environments.

Similarly, Ivor Goodson (1997) advocates a return to teacher-as-researcher model, where teacher professionalism is developed through collaboration with academics and reflection on both practice and theory, arguing for a reconceptualisation of educational research through collaboration between practitioners and academics so that teachers' voices are reinserted into the discourse of educational theory. This builds on earlier work (1993) where he argued for the acceptance on the part of the academy of the responsibility for sustaining and supporting teachers as researchers and for the focus of research to be placed squarely on the relationship between teachers work and their lives.

Elsewhere (Groundwater-Smith and Mockler 2006, 2008) we have developed the argument that practitioner research and research emanating from the academy share a 'different but equal' interrelationship, where a framework of ethics which cuts across issues of both validity and research quality in the case of practitioner research functions to underwrite quality considerations. Arguments about the legitimacy of action or practitioner research generally assume that this kind of local research claims the same scope and purpose as that which emanates from the academy, and thus seeks to measure what in fact equate with 'apples and oranges' on the same scale. We understand teacher research and research emanating from the academy to be different in their very constitution: where research emanating from the academy generally seeks, whether qualitative or quantitative in nature, whether broad in scope or confined to an individual case, to make a contribution to knowledge interests well beyond the site within which it is conducted. On the other hand, practitioner inquiry, while it may indeed make a broader contribution than the immediate context, is focused upon the development of *local* knowledge, contextualised professional development and learning for those who conduct the research and the community more broadly. The focus of contextualised and situational, and as such the work needs to be subjected to different, but no less rigorous, tests of quality. This focus on quality will be further taken up in Chapter 6.

Teacher and School as Knowledge Creator

The second emerging key issue is that of teacher and school as knowledge creator. In this section we argue that teachers and school communities have an essential role to play in the creation of new knowledge within and about education, an argument we will further develop in Chapter 4.

In their 1992 article entitled "Communities for Teacher Research: Fringe or Forefront?", Marilyn Cochran-Smith and Susan Lytle tackle the issue of structures which hinder and support teacher research, arguing that the flourishing of teacher research requires more than the provision of innovative structures - that the establishment and consolidation of intellectual communities for teacher research is necessary (Cochran-Smith and Lytle 1992). They argue that the remedy to obstacles to teacher research within schools, namely teacher isolation, occupational socialisation (after the work of Lortie 1975), the prevalence of a technical knowledge base (after Apple 1986) and accompanying epistemology and the prevailing reputation of educational research as irrelevant to the work of the teacher can only be arrested by the power of community. Furthermore, once established, such communities will not only 'add to the knowledge base on teaching, but their collective power as knowledge-generating communities is likely to influence broader school policies' (Cochran-Smith and Lytle 1992: 320).

This acceptance of the knowledge-building capabilities of schools and teachers is further developed in earlier work conducted by one of the authors of this book, who argued over a decade ago for the efficacy of practitioner research in school reform and improvement efforts, focusing on work carried out by members of the Australian National Schools Network (ANSN) in the 1990s (Groundwater-Smith

1998). In providing a framework for the conduct of teacher research, marrying classroom practitioners with academic researchers, and providing a forum for the publication and legitimisation of teacher research, she argues that the ANSN was engaged in fostering a culture of research within member schools. Groundwater-Smith focuses on the mutual benefits of involvement in such projects to both university-based participants and school-based professionals, in granting both 'the time and the space to listen and learn from each other' (p.33). She conceptualises the role of the university-based partner in this relationship to be one primarily related to providing 'research' expertise to help inform, highlight, gather information on and make problematic the aspects of education under investigation. This is not a relationship where the hierarchy of legitimacy places teacher knowledge in one place and academic knowledge in another. She is at pains to impress that '[a]ll those involved in the research have been enabled to challenge each other's analyses and interpretations' (1998: 27). Similarly, the work of the Coalition of Knowledge Building Schools in Australia has been well documented in this area (e.g. Groundwater-Smith and Mockler 2009, forthcoming; Mockler et al. 2005), and will be further elaborated in Chapter 11.

In his work on "The Knowledge-Creating School" (1999), David Hargreaves draws on literature surrounding notions of the learning organisation and knowledge management to argue for the need for schools to become knowledge-creating institutions. For Hargreaves, there can be no question around the ability of schools and teachers to engage in the activity of knowledge creation - he erects no epistemological boundaries around the notion of teachers' professional knowledge - although he concedes that the implications of what he terms to be a 'radical reconceptualisation of knowledge creation' (p.122) are largely to be felt by universities offering teacher 'training' programmes. Hargreaves employs Nonaka and Takeuci's model of knowledge creation in business (1995) as the basis for his model of the knowledge-creating school, which claims a distinction similar to that employed by Huberman (1996) between 'explicit' and 'tacit' knowledge to illustrate the creation of knowledge within an organisation. Further, Hargreaves employs the notion of teacher as 'tinker' (Huberman 1992), based on the work of Levi-Strauss and originally employed by Huberman to illustrate the inability of teachers to make a significant contribution to the creation of professional knowledge due to their lack of engineering skills and expert knowledge (Huberman 1996). Hargreaves claims that 'the tinkering teacher is an individualised embryo of institutionalised knowledge creation' (p.129), and further argues that there is a small step for teachers to take between 'tinkering' and the creation of professional knowledge. Having effectively used Huberman's own logic against him, Hargreaves' parting gesture is to throw the ball back into the universities' court, claiming that that the academy is responsible for the creation of knowledge-creating teachers and suggesting ways in which universities might begin going about the task. While we differ from Hargreaves in our firmly-held belief that the process of knowledge creation in education is appropriate within both the academy *and* schools, and that educational research need not necessarily be pragmatic and practical in its entirety, he does offer a sound perspective on the capability of schools as knowledge-creating organisations.

The ideas expressed by those who advocate for a knowledge-creating orientation for teachers and schools stand in stark contrast to those expounded by Huberman in the section above and Fenstermacher in the section below, where in both cases the knowledge-building capabilities of schools are denied in favour of the preservation of old discourses and traditional methods of knowledge creation. In this sense, both of the issues discussed so far connect to that of the legitimacy of teacher research, to which we now turn, and which will be further expanded subsequently in Chapter 4.

The Legitimacy of Teacher Research

In his 1994 discussion of teacher research, Fenstermacher draws a distinction between practical knowledge (that which is a product, in this case, of the teachers craft) and formal knowledge (that which, in his estimation, is a product of the academy), which he then uses as a tool to critique the efforts of teacher researchers, once again reinforcing the dichotomy of teacher versus academic researcher. Fenstermacher continues to claim a monopoly on 'knowledge' itself on behalf of the academy

> "...suggesting that an "unfortunate permissiveness arises" (1994: 41) when alternative sites of knowledge production, not subject to the regimes of justification and verification present within the academy, are legitimised."

Fenstermacher's argument serves to reinforce dominant and patriarchal paradigms of research and academia by insisting that teacher researchers conform to 'norms' of philosophy and epistemology in defining and developing a discourse which is fundamentally different from those that have gone before. Parallels to his argument can be found in academic writing from all disciplines which have been touched by feminist and other forms of post-structuralist analysis in the past 20 years.

Marilyn Cochran-Smith and Susan Lytle, have made a very significant contribution to the discussion of the legitimacy of teacher research, both in terms of their discussion of purposes and structures of teacher research and in their advancement of an epistemological framework for teacher research which is informed by their earlier employment of class, race and gender as categories of analysis in education. They argue that research paradigms applied to teachers' work effectively marginalise and exclude teachers' voices from the knowledge base for teaching, thus preventing teachers from involvement in the process of knowledge creation about their profession. They contend that teacher research is a valid and valuable form of educational research, both to teachers and academics, and argue against the basic comparison between school-based and university-based research on the grounds that it is these very comparisons which have contributed to the exclusion of teacher research from research on teaching generally. Their central point is that teacher research constitutes a separate, equally legitimate arena of knowledge about teaching, and that the opening up and exploration of the issues, which divide teacher research from research about teaching 'may help raise critical questions about the nature of knowledge for teaching and hence enhance research in both communities' (1990: 10).

In their 1993 work, Cochran-Smith and Lytle claim that 'teacher inquiry is a way for teachers to know their own knowledge' (1993: 45). They argue for the development of a new epistemology of teachers' work which allows for teachers to be creators of knowledge for and about their work. In this they link with our argument, made in Chapter 1, that teacher professional judgement, honed through the collection and analysis of evidence on a local level, is both critical to the profession and currently under threat from discourses of objectivity and standardisation. Their thesis here is that research emanating from an emic perspective actually functions to subvert the norms of inquiry, where 'subjective and local knowing rather than objectified and distanced "truth" is the goal' (1993: 58). Once again they argue for the acceptance of teacher research as a discourse different but nevertheless equal to those with their roots in the academy, and for the recognition of teachers as generators of knowledge within their field and the establishment of a 'grander arena that privileges local as well as public knowledge' (1993: 62). In a subsequent article, Cochran-Smith and Lytle rail against what they perceive to be the conservative backlash brought against the teacher research movement by the likes of Fenstermacher and Huberman. They conceptualise the teacher research movement as a challenge to 'the division of practitioners from researchers, doers from thinkers, actors from analysts, actions from ideas' (1998: 24) and argue for the acceptance of models of teacher research and professional knowledge as new iterations of old notions thus legitimately entitled to new discourses conceptualised as separate from the old. They claim that the questions raised by teacher researchers around notions of knowledge and power give rise to a stance on the part of conservative academics designed to preserve the 'hegemony of university-generated knowledge' and 'keep teachers 'in their place'' (1998: 27).

The field of inquiry-based teacher professional development, comprising action research, teacher research and their variants opens up questions of the relationship of the school to the academy, the ownership of knowledge and discourse around education and questions around the legitimacy of teacher research as a means to anything other than teacher professional development and improvement. The tensions would be greatly reduced if scholars were not tied to a bipolar dichotomy where teacher research is conceptualised as *the same as* research emanating from the academy, and thus subject to the same tests for validity and generalisability, or *different to* research emanating from the academy, where the immediate assumption is that the two must be unequal in status. Cochran-Smith and Lytle, and to some extent Sachs, have broken through this dichotomy to conceptualise teacher research as different but equal, as have the authors of this book in proposing differing measures of validity and quality for practitioner research, linked to ethics (Groundwater-Smith and Mockler 2006, 2008).

The Past 10 Years: Practitioner Inquiry as an Implementation Tool

David Hargreaves's 1996 Teacher Training Agency lecture entitled 'Teaching as a Research-Based Profession' heralded the arrival of an era where practitioner research has been often utilised as an implementation tool by governments and departments of education, particularly in the UK and Australia. Hargreaves lamented the lack of 'value for money' in publicly funded educational research and called for educational researchers to concentrate their efforts on 'what works' in the classroom, so as to systematically begin the codification of teachers technical knowledge and skill for the purpose of cataloguing and subsequently dispersing 'best practice' among the entire profession (Hargreaves, D. 1996). Part of a broader push towards compliance within education, the discourse of instrumentalism within which Hargreaves' thesis is situated, has emerged on three linked fronts, each with practical implications for teacher professional learning through the promotion of 'what works' in the classroom, namely educational research, 'evidence-based practice' and teacher education.

Hargreaves' key call was for teaching to become an 'evidence-based' profession such as medicine, where being 'evidence-based' is predicated upon a positivistic understanding of 'evidence' as leading to scientific certainty in relation to 'what works'. In a subsequent work, David Hargreaves writes in the context of a discussion of the impact of New Labour on the educational policy environment in the UK: 'However, there is another element in the new government's approach which gives rise to optimism, namely its pragmatic approach to 'what works' and to the rapid dissemination of 'good practice' throughout the education service' (Hargreaves, D. 1999: 245). A key to understanding Hargreaves' particular perspective on teachers and their work can perhaps best be found in his assertion that 'government can help [teachers adapt to change] by reconceptualising the role and professional identity of teachers and by providing conditions under which they can adapt successfully to these changes' (Hargreaves, D. 1998). The key assumption underpinning this statement, namely that teacher professionalism and teacher professional identity are tools for government control rather than teacher agency highlights the conservatism and narrowness of Hargreaves' arguments in relation to evidence-based practice and teacher professional development, and also pervades Hargreaves' other work (e.g. Hargreaves 1994).

The discourse of 'what works' has been roundly criticised, most vocally by scholars who have since been helpfully classified by Hargreaves as 'postmodern hermits' (1999: 242). Martyn Hammersley (1997), Tony Edwards (1996) and Harvey Goldstein (1996), for example, responded quickly with a critique of the narrow notions of 'evidence' upon which comparisons between education and medicine have been predicated, arguing that greater expenditure is the key to improving any deficiencies which may exist in educational research. Elizabeth Atkinson argued vehemently 'in defence of ideas', offering that 'a narrow focus on 'what works' will close the door that leads to new possibilities, new strategies, new ways of reframing and reconceiving the educational enterprise' (2000: 328). Jill Blackmore (2002) has applied the discussion to the Australian context, arguing that evidence-based practice, particularly the model derived from medicine, fails to capture the complexity of the educational field, especially with relation to the theory–practice dynamic and relationships between education policy, research and practice. Further, she argues for the employment of research-based policy and practice, albeit one which differs from Hargreaves' conceptualisation:

> Research based practice works through the theory practice dynamic critically, and it is that criticality that is crucial for a knowledge based democracy which takes into account the social and cultural as well as the scientific and technological. It requires researchers to problem set and not just problem solve, to be strategic as well as relevant. It requires from teachers as practitioner researchers another level of professional judgement that derives from the theoretical underpinnings of their disciplinary field of practice. (Blackmore 2002: 17)

As the ideology of 'what works' and the culture of compliance within education has gained traction over the past decade, inquiry-based professional learning, often badged as evidence-based practice, has become a preferred tool for implementation of government policy within classrooms. In the UK, the National Teacher Research Panel, formed in 1999, has three key goals:

- To ensure that all research in education takes account of the teacher perspective
- To ensure a higher profile for research and evidence-informed practice in government, academic and practitioner communities[1]
- To increase the number of teachers engaged in, and with the full spectrum of, research activity

The panel encourages teachers to engage in teacher research and evidence-based practice as part of continuing professional development, and as such their programmes articulate with the Advanced Skills Teacher process and a myriad of government-funded projects, which provide grants to schools for project work utilising action research methods.

In Australia, a similar focus is reflected in the Australian Government Quality Teacher Program (AGQTP), which since 1999 has provided funding for groups of teachers within schools to undertake collaborative projects organised around various government-determined agendas for professional learning. Action learning, the preferred approach for many iterations of the AGQTP, is presented as a more benign version of action research, lacking in the perceived methodological rigour assumed in the process of 'action research', as well as the critical social intent of action or teacher research. The observation by Stephen Kemmis with which this chapter began, that such forms of research 'may even have become a vehicle for domesticating students and teachers to conventional forms of schooling', emerges from the widespread adoption of such approaches to teacher inquiry.

---

[1]National Teacher Research Panel web site, http://www.standards.dfes.gov.uk/ntrp/ourwork/, Accessed 12 April 2008.

Our argument here is not that teacher research cannot be effectively used as a pathway for professional learning on a large scale utilising government funding, but rather that the appropriation of action research as a tool for implementing policy on a school and classroom level satisfies neither the critical social intent of the work nor the professional learning imperative. In order for such work to remain true to its historical and social roots and to also qualify as authentic inquiry-based professional learning, a number of conditions are necessary.

In terms of purpose and intent, authentic inquiry-based professional learning requires conditions where teachers determine the agenda and focus of the research in line with their concerns and their students' interests, where a problem-solving approach is met with a willingness to problematise aspects of practice and where the evidence is gathered and employed on a local level with links to the broader socio-political landscape of education. In terms of evidence and process, a methodological and ethical rigour is required, such that participants in the process are accountable and responsible to each other for decisions made and actions taken, and where the evidence is collected, organised and analysed in a collaborative and transparent way. Issues of reliability and validity are significant here. In terms of action and effect, it requires a commitment on the part of the school community to support practitioner researchers in their capacity to disseminate and act upon findings in such a way that an authentic and critical response is made which honours the participants and the research endeavour itself. An embrace of the work as a 'vehicle for educational critique' (Kemmis 2006: 459), where real findings feed into real changes for students and teachers, regardless of the discomfort they may bring, is inherent in this condition.

Conclusion

Inquiry-based professional learning, as we observed in the introduction to this chapter, has burgeoned in the past decade as a tool for teachers' professional learning, but enjoys a long, trans-national heritage and history. In Chapter 8, we will explore at length the conditions and contexts for effective inquiry-based professional learning, and subsequently, in the case studies which form Chapters 10 and 11, examples of inquiry-based professional learning emanating from conditions such as these will be further elaborated. These conditions build upon the historical roots of action research, practitioner inquiry and teacher research, and privilege the critical orientation which has been discussed at length in this chapter. Such an approach cuts 'against the grain' in this age of compliance, and requires of school leaders, teacher educators and teachers themselves a significant measure of personal and professional courage. It is to this notion of courage that we now turn.

Chapter 3
Developing Courage

Trust is a little like air–we pay little attention to it until it is not there.

(Hoy and Tarter 2004: 252)

Why begin a chapter that is concerned with the development of professional courage by making a reference to trust? Trust requires us to expose ourselves to our professional peers. We shall argue that trust itself takes courage because in its manifestation it is necessary that we acknowledge our vulnerabilities, our sensibilities and our frailties. It is difficult to trust our colleagues and for them to trust us if we mask who we are and what it is that we believe. Hoy and Tarter (2004) in the article from which the quote is taken argue that trust is fundamental to organisational justice in schools. We would go further and claim that it is *courage*, which allows trust to grow and flourish, that is the bedrock of professional collegiality whether in schools or academic institutions such as universities. We are, in effect, deeply interested in notions of how courage can be manifest in our behaviours as educators, in particular, in relation to being educators with a mission to investigate with honesty and integrity the circumstances of our practice. Like trust, we pay little attention to courage until it is not there.

One might argue that courage has always been required of dedicated educators; courage to commit themselves fully to their practice and all that it entails. However, we assert that in this age of compliance, which presses upon practitioners to conform to the wishes and edicts of others, it becomes an essential feature of teachers' work. Engaging in inquiry can unveil uncomfortable truths and reveal policies and procedures that may not be in the best interests of either students or their teachers.

Perspectives on Courage

This chapter will focus on a number of perspectives on courage in relation to teacher professional learning, many of which were referred to in our opening chapters, these being:

S. Groundwater-Smith and N. Mockler, *Teacher Professional Learning in an Age of Compliance*, DOI: 10.1007/978-1-4020-9417-0_3,
© Springer Science + Business Media B.V. 2009

- The courage to have a concern for procedural justice
- The courage to engage with teaching's moral purpose
- The courage to be truly professional in undertaking practice
- The courage to be progressive and take a transformative and libratory stance
- The courage to tolerate ambiguity
- The courage to have hope
- The courage to ask the difficult questions and
- The courage to propose the challenging solutions

Courage and Procedural Justice

We begin by asking ourselves what we understand procedural justice to be. We argue that in effect it is justice that is directed to moral outcomes, guided by social norms and principles. As Nussbaum (2001) observed in relation to the work of John Rawls:

> People need norms to guide them, in both personal and political life. And it seems reasonable to suggest, especially in the political life of a democracy, that we ought to deliberate together about the principles that guide us. (Nussbaum 2001: 1)

The social norms that we have in mind are the need for fairness and clarity in the various roles and tasks that are undertaken in our schools and universities; the right to a voice, including that of those who dissent; and a recognition and respect for difference. Too often, in our minds there is a significant 'gap' between these aspirations and what takes place in learning institutions. Roles and responsibilities may be arbitrarily distributed, or based upon the preferences and predilections of those holding the greatest power. Those who might wish to debate or argue the ways in which the various procedures have evolved may be silenced, often by colleagues who would prefer not to 'rock the boat'. Building a diverse, adaptive and socially responsible workplace may require walking a tightrope between conformity and rebellion (Meyerson 2008), but there come times when compromise is untenable, when less popular ideas deserve attention and careful scrutiny. Being different should not render one the butt of mockery and derision. Paying attention to procedural justice undoubtedly takes courage.

Courage and Teaching's Moral Purpose

For us teaching's most fundamental moral purpose is that it makes a difference to the good for the young people in our schools.[1] This entails engaging in authentic

---

[1] From this point on in the chapter, our attention will be directed towards schools. However, we wish to recognise that much of what is written counts also for higher education.

change measures rather than remaining satisfied with the *status quo*. It connotes, as Fullan (2006: 114) puts it 'pushing further into ... action poetry'. For Fullan, this means having a commitment to raising the bar and closing the gap in student achievement, treating people with respect and having an orientation to more broadly improving the educational environment. For us it also encompasses the need and desirability to build social capital in our schools. Social capital is the means whereby members of a community build trust through cooperation within and between groups. It is a way of distributing knowledge and information that can lead to well-being through civic engagement and the development of a cohesive community. Building social capital is an antidote to the anxiety and hostility that Pfeffer and Sutton (2000) discuss in their book *The Knowing-Doing Gap* where they found a pervasive atmosphere of fear and distrust in those organisations that were incapable of bridging the knowing and doing chasm.

To make a difference in young people's lives is a considerable challenge in many of our schools where those lives are led under disabling and often traumatic circumstances, or alternatively where they are so cushioned by affluence and materialism that the members of the school community have little capacity for empathy and concern for others. When designing investigations into school practices, a question to be considered will be 'who benefits from this and how?' with, of course, the corollary also in mind 'at whose cost?' An action-based inquiry that supports the learning of some, but pays the price of denying decent conditions for others can scarcely be one that satisfies a moral purpose. As teachers in England, for example, struggle to meet externally imposed 'targets' by increasing the prospects of some students attaining higher results they may well be tempted to pour resources into that group's needs at the expense of those in both higher and lower bands of achievement—a matter further discussed in Chapter 6. In fact it was reported in the Education Guardian (2006) that teachers are prioritising targets over study skills. These strategies to maintain a place in the country's league tables is impacting upon teacher's health and well-being as they struggle to maintain their professional judgement in the face of externally imposed policies. It certainly requires personal fortitude to resist such strategies.

In sum, we assert that teaching's moral purpose is necessarily a political project. As we indicated in the Chapter 2 the heritage of teacher as researcher is derived from the early manifestations of action research that was designed as a tactic for social change. The processes are, in effect, professional ones requiring integrity and wisdom in the knowledge that what is known or not known about practice is always incomplete.

The Courage to Be Truly Professional in Undertaking Practice

The legal profession has a term 'reduction to practice' in patent and intellectual property law where the implication is that practice is a simple synthesis. We prefer to think about 'elevation to practice' which recognises that the doing of work in education is complex and grows from a sense of vocation, requiring practitioners to be truly professional rather than merely conforming to standards of professionalism invoked through various accrediting agencies.

The fact that teacher's professional work has changed over the years is unarguable. Those changing conditions have been neatly summed up by Ballet, Kelchtermans and Loughran (2006) as a form of intensification. They argue that teachers are working harder and smarter, and are being driven by more and more demanding community expectations. They strive to comply with the rules and regulations determined by policy makers and various governing bodies, as well as by the high norms that they commit to themselves. Connell (2007) also reports that teachers are working longer and harder as they take on additional roles and responsibilities in line with changing social conditions. Furthermore, in common with many other workplaces, information and communication technologies with their ongoing convergences are also contributing to intensification. In being truly professional in their practice in general and when undertaking inquiry in particular educators are taking on a formidable role, all the more so when they have an aspiration to challenge a prevailing educational climate that is trending to conservative practice.

Too often professionalism is taken to mean the capacity to satisfy the technical aspects of the work of teaching–a mastery of content knowledge (itself problematic); an ability to manage unruly behaviour; having sound communication strategies and other such skills. Important as these attributes are, there are equally important professional interests that should be held to account such as having the intellectual tools to interpret the complexities of students' lives, or the ways in which power and authority are managed within the individual school and the system that manages it. The nature of teacher professionalism is contested; it is forever situated in the prevailing discourses of the day.

The Courage to Be Progressive and Take a Transformative and Libratory Stance

As we observed in our opening chapter, neoliberal and neoconservative political agendas are at work in the USA, the UK and Australia. Although in the latter case, with a recent change of the federal government, we may see some policy change, it remains likely that the trend to consolidate state-based school curriculum, testing and reporting into national systems will continue. It seems that successive generations can seize upon new and innovative ideas such as open classrooms, student-centred learning, integrated curriculum, authentic assessment, new literacies and the like, well grounded as these practices may be, only to be trammelled by 'common-sense approaches to education' (Groundwater-Smith et al. 2007: 44). These grow from a perspective that everyone is an 'expert' in what schools should do. And, in the main, what schools should do is reproduce a one-size-fits-all education that will allow standardised testing and national comparisons. In such a context it is critical that stories of progressive and libratory practices that have been successfully enacted be told. As Apple so compellingly puts it:

Although 'public storytelling' may not be sufficient it informs an important function. It
keeps alive and reminds ourselves of the very possibility of difference in an age of audits,
commodification and disrespect. (2006:122)

Good stories that make compelling reading are not merely unproblematised narratives,
they are ones that draw our attention to the complexities and ambiguities inherent in
all social practices.

The Courage to Tolerate Ambiguity

For many, schools are seen to be places that should peddle unambiguous 'knowledge',
that is, sites where knowledge is uncontestable. There is one way to solve a math-
ematical equation; one procedure for undertaking a scientific experiment; one way
to analyse history; and one way to read a book or play. Across the English-speaking
world, for example, there has been a shift to a more traditional approach to teaching
literature as a result of political pressure, mainly exercised through the print media
and talkback radio. Rather than tolerating ambiguity, these powerful voices
promote the inviability of the text. Snyder (2008) in her powerful book *The Literacy
Wars* explores how literacy has become a vicious battleground in Australia. New
literacies that include paying attention to social and electronic media are seemingly
not to be taught in our schools, which should return to the old cannons and one
preferred form of grammar.

Treating ambiguity, itself, as an object of study worthy of consideration is a
relatively new practice in our schools. It requires learners, whether they be the
students or teachers, to be prepared to take a critical position wherein they articulate
and defend their arguments and address the rules of engagement. They are transformed from being passive receivers of rules to beings finders and evaluators. They
seek to find a foothold in a world that is increasingly intensified, individualised and
accelerated (Giddens 2002).

All this requires a degree of social activism previously rarely to be found in
education.

The Courage to Have Hope

These manifestations of courage should not be taken to be behaviours that are
wholly defensive in the light of today's prevalence of conservative political regimes.
We also advocate the need and indeed the right to hope. Hope is energising. Its *sine
qua non* is fear and despair. For us it is essential that teachers have hope-among
other things: hope to make improvements in the lives of young people; hope to
develop in them the skills, competencies and attributes that will help them to grow
into decent adults; and hope that their professional work is understood and
respected in the community and within the schools themselves.

One of the most remarkable stories of hope and courage comes to us from half a century ago. Some years ago one of us was visiting a friend in Oslo. We went to Norway's Resistance Museum that was established in 1966 as an independent foundation for the purpose of contributing to the presentation of an authentic picture of the occupation by means of objects, pictures, printed matter, etc. These were exhibited with a view to giving the young people of the day and coming generations a trustworthy account of the great difficulties represented by occupation and foreign rule.

Many such museums are scattered around the world that have experienced such great tribulation; so what made it so special and why should we invoke the memory here in a discussion of hope and trust in the context of education? In the museum there is one particularly poignant section devoted to the resistance of Norwegian teachers to the fascist 'minister-President', Vidkun Quisling, who set out to establish the Corporative State on Mussolini's model, selecting teachers as the first 'corporation'. For this he created a new teacher's organisation with compulsory membership and a requirement that they follow a so-called Aryan curriculum.

The underground called on the teachers to resist. Between 8,000 and 10,000 of the country's 12,000 teachers wrote letters to Quisling's Church and Education Department. All signed their names along with addresses to the wording. Each teacher said he or she could neither assist in promoting fascist education of the children nor accept membership in the new teacher's organisation. The government threatened them with dismissal and closed all schools for a month. Many were arrested. Teachers held classes in private homes. Despite censorship, news of the resistance spread. Tens of thousands of letters of protest from parents poured into the government office.

On cattle car trains and overcrowded steamers, the arrested teachers were shipped to the far north. They were kept at Kirkenes in miserable conditions, doing dangerous work. However, their suffering strengthened morale on the home front and posed problems for Quisling's regime. As Quisling once raged at the teachers in a school near Oslo: 'You teachers have destroyed everything for me!' Fearful of alienating Norwegians still further, Quisling finally ordered the teachers' release. Eight months after the arrests, the last teachers returned home to triumphal receptions. They had restored hope in a regime of fear and loathing.

Teachers in our schools today continue to have hope that they may teach as they know best and that what they teach is continuously open to debate and discussion.

The Courage to Ask the Difficult Questions

We do not lightly turn to issues of debate. To be passive, quiet and still may be far more comfortable than to open any particular Pandora's box. Let us take the example of bullying. It may be agreed, as a school-based inquiry project, to examine more thoroughly issues around bullying in all of its manifestations, between and among students. Today bullying and violence in schools is often associated in people's minds with physical encounters, generally found among boys. However, bullying for girls, while different in nature can be just as deleterious in its consequences and often takes indirect forms such as spreading rumours, using electronic media and ostracising particular students from the favoured group. Social exclusion and marginalisation can be hurtful to both young boys and girls who do not have a robust self-image. The means for practising such exclusion can be covert and difficult to detect.

But what if the bullying is not confined to the students? What happens when a young person observes 'but teachers bully too; they bully us and they bully each other!' In an Australian National Safe Schools Best Practice Project undertaken by one of the authors of this book just such a matter arose. Students spoke of the social manipulation that they observed among the teachers. While it became evident that there was a bullying culture in the school that went well beyond the ways in which the students interacted with one another, it was denied by the staff. The difficult question regarding the overall bullying environment was not to be investigated on the pretext that it was not a question raised in the original project proposal.

Asking difficult questions of ourselves and our colleagues can expose vulnerabilities that some may prefer to put aside. Furthermore, those questions can themselves be generative of solutions that may be unsettling and discomforting.

The Courage to Propose the Challenging Solutions

Of course proposing challenging solutions assumes that the difficult question has been asked. Let us hypothesise for a moment that the issue of staff bullying had arisen and been investigated, what kinds of solutions would it have been possible to put forward? Perhaps a staff ombudsperson who could investigate bullying allegations and suggest forms of reconciliation between staff could be appointed. But by whom? What would the processes be? How could confidentiality be observed? What conditions would be established for a right of reply? Developing genuinely challenging solutions would certainly require a steady set of nerves, not just on the part of the individual but within the whole organisation. This brings us to the large, overarching question for this chapter, that is, in an age so remarkable for its compliance requirements how do we maintain our courage?

Courage and Compliance

'Compliance' could well be one of Don Watson's Weasel Words. In his book *Watson's Dictionary of Weasel Words* (2004) one of Australia's most formidable speech writers explores the manipulation of language by those in power. He argues that they are the words with which bureaucrats and ideologues are entranced. They are selected as words that hide the truth in the form of codes and clichés. The dictionary

meaning of compliance is relatively straightforward; it is the state or act of conforming or agreeing to do something. Teachers are asked to supervise students in
bus lines; they comply-that is they agree to undertake the responsibility. There is no
sense of coercion or sanctions. However, today compliance has become attached to
a much stronger legalistic regime. Various regulatory frameworks are developed,
some designed for the social good to curb unconscionable conduct such as price
fixing, others as a means of social control often designed to assist large organisations
and bureaucracies in managing risk. One might argue, for instance, that much of the
occupational health and safety regulations that are so pervasive in government
organisations contribute little to the social good. Teachers now find that to take
children out of school, to visit museums, stay overnight at camps or go on a
bushwalk often requires more paperwork than the experience merits.

We would argue, as a central premise of this book, that compliance does not
necessarily mean good governance in the management of educational practices. We
see that teachers should have the professional responsibility to weigh up given situations and determine the most appropriate course of action, working of course
within the law. Take, for example, the matter of child protection and access to the
Internet in schools, as Sachs and Mellor (2003) have pointed out in relation to risk
management and child protection 'the duty of care has become careful duty' (p.12).
By merely inserting 'child protection' and 'the Internet' into a search engine, over
two million citations appeared in 0.22 s. Clearly, fear has been instilled into the
community to the extent that a kind of paralysis can ensue. Young people find sites
on school computers are more often blocked than not. Of course, no one is going
to argue for untrammelled access that would expose young people to danger and
unwelcome attention, but it may be that a more trusting regime needs to be established, such that young users themselves have some agency and sense of responsibility
for what they use and how they use it.

Seemingly in their efforts to control and manage practitioners education authorities
take as the default model that teachers are rational professionals concerned with
deterrence, rather than virtuous professionals concerned with justice-the kind of
activist professionals of whom Sachs (2003) writes. Newman (2006:10) goes
further and recommends that teachers should be taught defiance:

> Our job is to help people become truly conscious, understand the different worlds we live
> in and develop a morality in the face of the evident amorality of our universe. It is to teach
> people how to make up their own minds, and how to take control of their moment. It is to
> teach choice. It is to help ourselves and others break free from our pasts, plan for the
> futures we want and resist the futures we do not want. Our job is to teach defiance.

So, is it at all possible to break or bend the rules, to engage in forms of educational
practice that transcend compliance, to be courageous in the face of ever-increasing
regulation? Later in this book we shall discuss extended cases; here, we wish to
draw upon a recent development in school-based inquiry that does step outside
some of the perceived boundaries and limitations placed upon such investigations-
that is, the exploration of small studies, which have employed the notion of 'student
voice', where the young people themselves make a substantial and meaningful contribution to the research and action. These may not, of themselves, be revolutionary. But

they are examples of risk-taking and trust, of stepping out beyond the strictures of compliance.

Listening and Acting on Student Voice

We do not intend, at this juncture, to make the case for researching with young people. This matter will be more fully covered in Chapter 7. Suffice to say, there is now a growing literature in the area, much of which is summed up in the special issue of *Discourse*, 28 (3) 2007. Rather, we wish to turn to two recent studies by Bland and Atweh (2007) and Johnson (2007). We have selected them because they show some hallmarks of resisting current trends for professional learning to be conducted within large, funded programmes and because they demonstrate that learning can be initiated and inspired by young people themselves.

Derek Bland and Bill Atweh undertook an evaluation of a students-as-researchers project in Brisbane, Australia. They argued that the use of participatory action research provides a process by which marginalised students, their teachers and university academics can work collaboratively to make positive gains for young people. The project extended across a full school year and incorporated workshops at the university campus and meetings of the various research groups at the participating schools. The students were seen as particularly powerful 'insiders' (p.341) in that they were able to provide extensive and long-term knowledge of the various conditions that affected them and would therefore be well placed as researchers. They were able, for example, to identify aspects of racism manifest not only by other students, but also by some teachers that contributed to indigenous students choosing to leave school early. The students devised action strategies such as creating a room for indigenous students as a retreat and tuition centre (p.343).

The study pointed to some of the significant problematics encountered when students are engaged as researchers, such as:

- Adjusting from being marginalised to being consulted
- Needing to find a new place in the power dynamics of the school
- Not being co-opted into reproducing the existing orthodoxies in practice
- Learning to speak usefully, responsibly and intelligibly
- Being prepared to move outside 'safe' areas for discussion
- Finding strategies that can contribute to a working consensus[2]

We chose to draw attention to this particular study because we believe that it is one that would have taken a deal of courage on the part of all who participated. To disclose racism is always a challenging task, especially when it is being expressed by those seen to be holding significant power. University academics would have been sensitive to the relational difficulties between themselves, the teachers and the young people and might, at times have preferred to step aside from these tensions.

---

[2] This list is our synthesis of the discussion in the paper, pp. 344–346.

All would have had to deal with the legal and ethical constraints placed upon them by different parties and interests.

The second study to which we wish to draw attention is Kaye Johnson's investigation with much younger children regarding the nature of their learning and leisure environments in the school (Johnson 2007). The study was an attempt to redress the silencing of children regarding their everyday school lives. In its action research phase, young people conferred in four Values in Action (VIA) groups; these being: respect, fairness, mutual trust and social cohesion (p.40). These groups were charged with the overall responsibility of ensuring that the inquiries were conducted under the kinds of conditions spelled out by Bland and Atweh.

A significant part of the process was that the children would present their evidence and analysis to members of the School's Governing Council. One such presentation was with regard to 'Toilet Trouble' that demonstrated unhygienic, unpleasant facilities and unacceptable behaviour that happened in and around the school toilets leading to anxiety and refusal. Another group investigated what had become a less-than-inviting environment around the school's swimming pool. It takes considerable courage for such young people to argue so strenuously for improvement and change without adult intercession. They were required to face the fact that the Governing Council itself was constrained by economic and regulatory factors and to be judicious in their use of persuasive argument such that it facilitated rather than impeded decision making. In effect, they were learning something about *Realpolitik*, about being modest rather than overzealous and about having clear goals and strategies to reach them.

We might argue that in both of these cases the young people were exercising courage in its many manifestations as outlined earlier in this chapter. They were not *being good* as individuals, they were *doing good* as a community.

Conclusion

If we take doing research in schools as a form of work, as argued by Hodkinson (2004) and work as an opportunity to learn, then it follows that the kind of inquiry that will be generative and allow the doing of good must be such that there are real possibilities to learn. Authentic professional learning takes courage: first of all, it requires a recognition of the complexity of school education and then a desire for improvement and action. Of course we are mindful that the words 'improvement' and 'action' can themselves have the kind of weasel connotations that we discussed earlier in the chapter. Who can forget that the Scottish Clearances so poignantly evoked by Prebble (1969) were undertaken in the name of improvement where callous landowners set about reorganising the Highland landscape, agriculture and crofter life to conform to their own ideas of efficiency and progress? So, wishing for improvement and action must always be considered in the context of moral purpose as we have emphasised throughout the discussion thus far-a moral purpose that can contribute to the learning of all.

Finally, learning itself can be an uncomfortable enterprise. Sometimes it means going beyond a prevailing sentiment that schools should be consensual organisations where policies and practices are agreed upon through a process of collaborative decision making. But what happens when there is no agreement? In this chapter we have argued for the use of superordinate principles that transcend merely reaching consensus that is in itself an end, rather than a means. Thus, deliberative processes in decision making must accord with the kinds of procedural justice and moral purpose argued for at the beginning of this chapter. As Gutmann and Thompson (1996:4) have argued, '[d]eliberation is not only a means to an end, but also a means for deciding what means are morally required to pursue our common ends'.

Clearly, the interests and beliefs of those many persons engaged in educational practice cannot be seen to be identical, but it is essential that there is sufficient individual and organisational courage to go beyond 'the majority will rule'. The significant professional lesson to be learned, then, is to exhaustively explore what is possible and find a means for arriving at solutions to intransigent problems that can themselves remain open for later consideration. Gaps and fissures may be temporarily closed or bridged, but there always remains the possibility that they can reopen and reconfigure.

Part II
Professional Knowledge Building:
Tenets and Tools

Chapter 4
Mode 3 Knowledge: What It Is and Why We Need It

'Please would you tell me,' said Alice, a little timidly, for she was not quite sure whether it was good manners for her to speak first, 'why your cat grins?'

'It's a Cheshire Cat,' said the Duchess, 'and that's why.'

...

'I didn't know that Cheshire Cats always grinned; in fact, I didn't know that cats COULD grin.'

'They all can,' said the Duchess; 'and most of 'em do,'

'I don't know any that do,' Alice said very politely, feeling quite pleased to have got into the conversation.

'You don't know much,' said the Duchess; 'and that's a fact.'

(Carroll 1946*)*

Throughout *Alice's Adventures in Wonderland* the matter of knowledge and Alice's lack of it is a constant source of wonderment to her newly met companions. Characters expect her to know things of which she has had no experience and, not surprisingly, she is often bewildered.

When we speak of 'knowing' something in Education, it too can be bewildering. To what are we referring? Is it knowing how young people in our schools learn about civics and citizenship? Or is it knowing the ways in which the historical circumstances of schooling have developed in different contexts or economies? Or, perhaps, is it knowing how to structure teacher education to meet the new demands of Web2.0 technologies? When we start to scope the nature of professional knowledge building in as diverse and widespread a practice of education, it becomes clear that the field is governed by so many variables as to be vast, with some corners immensely fertile and well cultivated, while others are virtually uncharted. For this reason we cannot hope to discuss the professional knowledge itself, although we have already aired the notion of schools themselves being knowledge-creating

S. Groundwater-Smith and N. Mockler, *Teacher Professional Learning in an Age of Compliance*, DOI: 10.1007/978-1-4020-9417-0_4,
© Springer Science + Business Media B.V. 2009

organisations in Chapter 2. Rather, in this chapter we are interested in exploring how such knowledge has been accumulated, evaluated and subjected to critique and debate. We shall seek to blur the boundaries between those who are understood to be the producers and those who are the users of professional knowledge in terms of their functions and the esteem that is attached to them.

In their seminal work *The New Production of Knowledge* Gibbons et al. (1994) argue that knowledge production has been transformed. They distinguish between Mode 1 knowledge that is generated within the academy, or research establishments, through the filter of the disciplines and Mode 2 knowledge that is created in broader, transdisciplinary social and economic contexts. Basic to an understanding of the distinction are the ways in which the norms and conventions of each contribute to the manner in which problems are set and solved and the solutions judged and distributed. As well, the case is made for an interaction between Mode 1 and Mode 2 knowledge, 'specialists trained in the disciplinary sciences do enter Mode 2 knowledge production' (p.9) with some choosing to engage more and more within the context of application.

Importantly, Gibbons et al. subscribed to the principle that in whichever mode the knowledge was produced through research, whether basic or applied, it was in the hands of some kind of research community. The mutability of the research rested in its academic flexibility rather than that it might have emerged from the field itself. As we have observed (Groundwater-Smith and Mockler 2006) more recently, Nowotny, Scott and Gibbons (2003) have argued that judging the worth of the Mode 2 knowledge is no longer the exclusive province of the academy 'because there is no longer a stable taxonomy of codified disciplines from which "peers" can be drawn' (p.187). Indeed, they continue by asserting that the 'research game' is being joined by more and more players. Problem generation and problem solving are contextualised within professional practice in the face of 'variously jostling publics' (Nowotny et al., 2003, p.192). All the same, while the knowledge may not be discipline-based or generated from within the academy, Mode 2 knowledge still remains the province of the privileged who have the resources and capacity to publish through recognised media, whether journal articles, books or refereed conference papers.

In this chapter, we shall argue that as teacher research increases and the social technologies in digital space burgeon it is time to think even about the possibility of Mode 3 knowledge emerging. For the time being, though, we are interested in exploring how Mode 1 and Mode 2 knowledge came to dominate professional practice in education and how it has been increasingly questioned as those engaged in professional practice came to develop practice-based knowledge, particularly through the work of systematic practitioner inquiry.

Mode 1 and Mode 2 Knowledge as They Apply to Professional Practice in Education

For some time, in spite of the admonitions of Dewey as set out by Marshall (1984), there has been a persistent belief that there is a form of objectivist knowledge that is the result of certain kinds of research. Educational problems have been thought to be technical and therefore could be solved by applying the results of positivist research obtained in the best of all worlds via randomised control trials (Shavelson and Towne 2002). Thus, solving intractable problems would be resolved through the rational application of research outcomes. Professional practice could be prescribed and would be communicated through the agency of the social scientists whether working within Mode 1 or Mode 2 research communities. The assumed professional learning model was one of transmission; would-be practitioners were instructed regarding the research results that were rarely made problematic and then advised of ways in which they should teach a particular skill such as the acquisition of numeracy, or develop the appropriate content knowledge within various designated subjects such as Ancient History, or be advised of the best ways in which to manage classroom behaviour - all in spite of the possibility of multiple and at times contradictory solutions being offered by competing researchers. As we argued in Chapter 2, the 'what works' agenda, as espoused by David Hargreaves (1996) where he called for teaching to become an evidence-based profession, can result in the unproblematic acceptance of particular kinds of scientific evidence and clearly does not consider the more forensic approach that is advocated by those with an affiliation to practitioner inquiry.

All the same, the proliferation of research orientations is not necessarily to be considered a negative effort, as Lather (2006) argues a multiplicity of research paradigms can be studied for their consequences for practice. In writing of research training for students within the academy she posits:

> Across the paradigms, students trained in the philosophical, ethical and political values that undergird knowledge production will be able to negotiate the constantly changing landscape of educational research far beyond the application of technical methods and procedures. Layering complexity, foregrounding problems, thinking outside easy intelligibility and transparent understanding, the goal is to move educational research in many different directions in the hope that more interesting and useful ways of knowing will emerge. (p.53)

This may certainly be so for the formal study of research methods, however, for practitioners in the field the effect can be confusion and uncertainty. Nowhere has this been more manifest than in the literacy debates with researchers and scholars appealing to one research paradigm or another. On the one hand, there are the advocates of the teaching of reading principally through the employment of systematic phonic attack such as the case reported by Rose (2006) with the emphasis upon explicit letter and blend recognition and drawing upon a positivist research base. On the other hand, there are those who strongly support the notion of reading for pleasure as a means of gaining a breakthrough to literacy with reported outcomes related to enhanced reading and writing attainment (Clark and Rumbold 2006) and principally drawing upon qualitative inquiries. Each of these major recently published reports makes a case based upon peer-reviewed research with extensive reference lists to back their claims. Between them there are over 170 references to the research literature; however, there is only one researcher common to both. Rose's references tend to cite Mode 1 researchers with most being members of university communities, Clark and Rumbold's are more eclectic and cite the work of a range of organisations, thus drawing on Mode 2 professional knowledge production.

So what are practitioners in the field to make of this professional knowledge and how can they use it to enhance their practice? It is our belief that the gap, not only between the two Modes of knowledge production, but also between researchers and the field is so great that in effect teachers prefer to draw upon their own experience and 'know-how' to make decisions about how they will go about teaching reading. In spite of government edicts determining how literacy should be taught, often influenced by polemicists such as Kevin Donnelly in Australia (Donnelly 2004), teachers subvert the policies in order to enhance their students' opportunities. They use the wisdom of experience to mix and match their methods, not always with the best of results.

But making this case is only a very small part of the story. Over the years areas of research quite unfamiliar to teachers are being invoked as a means of persuading them that they should rethink practice. While teachers may feel confident about challenging specific reading research they are less comfortable when addressing 'grand' theories and the ways that they are evoked by the academy. Knowledge is not some sort of portable self-contained *thing* that may be transmitted by technically controlled conduits, but is socially constructed and located in socio-historical space. The process of meaning-making both of and from information is central, but it is also unsettling. Part of the role of the academic in conversation with the field is to disturb cherished ideas and beliefs. Nowhere is this more important than when addressing some of the 'grand theories' that as Bernstein (1983) put it are too often seen to 'provide a stable and reliable rock upon which we can secure our thought and action' (p.19). The way forward, he posited, is to recover the hermeneutic dimension that emphasises understanding and interpretation and locate these in socio-historical space. Thus, knowing about a particular theory or piece of research is not itself a sufficient basis for action. Indeed Kemmis and Conlon argue that transformation of practice must always be 'morally-informed committed action' (p.3). In other words, resulting social change must always consider the question of whose interests are being served.

It is at this intersection that the conversation between the academy and the field can be seen to be particularly powerful. In a recent discussion with Wilfred Carr[1] it was suggested that theory is often 'the plaything of practice'. Over the years particular theories gain an ascendancy: behaviourism, developmental psychology, constructivism, as have conditions such as postmodernity − their associated vocabularies find their way into policies: 'reinforcement', 'accommodation', 'scaffolding', 'deconstruction' − often with little or no critique. The theories themselves become transient and trivialised. And yet, having an explicit theory of practice is more than mere words. It provides a capacity to develop and evaluate action.

This brings us to a third way of thinking about professional knowledge, what we shall call Mode 3 knowledge.

---

[1] Recently he was in Australia as a visiting scholar at both the University of Sydney and the Charles Sturt University. The conversation was not documented, but I have requested his permission to quote the phrase that follows.

Mode 3 Knowledge Production: Opening Up the Field

Information about what and how to teach is burgeoning exponentially, not only through the media of academic writing and text book publishing but, most particularly, through Web2.0 technologies. Old models of transmission of professional knowledge are no longer sufficient for practitioners in our schools today, or indeed in other places where they may learn. As Cornu (2004) has observed, knowledge is now networked and requires an understanding of a collective intelligence over and above individual enterprise. Professional learning is now occurring in a contemporary world where the digital media increase exponentially day by day, constantly morphing into new forms, or as Alexander (2006) puts it a 'churning wave' (p.42). At no time in our human history has there been the capacity to connect and engage in what Jenkins, Clinton, Purushotma, Robinson and Weigel (2006) have called a participatory culture.

Self-publishing online no longer requires advanced technological skills; instead, it requires a will and a desire to communicate. Siemens (2006) provides a demonstration of ways in which substantial work on the nature of digitally mediated knowledge production is possible. Indeed, he argues that the very word 'production' implies something that is 'static', 'hard' and 'organised'; the product is created and flows from the creator to the receiver. Now, with the employment of blogs, wikis and the like, the flows are multidirectional, and the user is also the producer - new networks are being constantly formed and new pathways are created. Paradoxically, this cacophony of sources of information brings us back to some of the challenges that lie as that information is transformed into personal knowledge, a process that in turn can be said to be a form of learning.

Green and Hannon (2006) have suggested that there are four key components to learning: finding information and knowledge, doing something with it, sharing it with an audience and reflecting on it. But as Lawrence Stenhouse (1979a) in a pre-digital world reminded us, information and knowledge are two different things: 'Information is not knowledge until the factor of error in it is appropriately estimated' (quoted in Stenhouse 1983: 141). However, here is the rub, estimating error is not easily undertaken alone - it is something that requires social interaction as ideas are explored and arguments are developed and justified.

Eraut and Hirsh (2007) distinguish between forms of knowledge rather differently. They believe the narrowest definition to be what they call *codified knowledge* (p.5), that which is stored in books and journals and contrast it to *uncodified cultural knowledge*, which is acquired informally through participation in the working practices of the organisation and which contributes to the formation of *personal knowledge*.[2]

Since they believe that personal knowledge comes from observation and experience they see it to be '*holistic* rather than *fragmented*' (p.6) and are able to produce *capability*.

---

[2]All italicised phrases are such in the original text.

Although they ultimately eschew the term, we could argue that such knowledge is 'personal knowledge' and that it comes about through both tacit and explicit social interactions. Either way, Eraut in his influential book *Developing Professional Knowledge and Competence* (1994) argues that professional knowledge cannot be characterised independently of how it has been learned and how it is used.

Mode 3 knowledge production, in the end, will be as much about social interaction in both the virtual and actual world as about the tabling of the information in the first place. It is about what Castells (2001) calls 'power networking'.

> This power networking is changing the way we perceive, organise, manage, produce, consume, fight and counter-fight – embracing practically all dimensions of social life. The interaction between the revolution in information technology, the process of globalisation and the emergence of networking as the predominant social form of organization constitutes a new social structure: the network society. (p.548)

It is clear that in contrast to the development of Mode 1 and Mode 2 knowledge, we are now in a professional environment that is being increasingly democratised. Professionals are finding their own ways to organise, evaluate and disseminate information that bypasses traditional forms. However, knowledge created in this way is not without its critics.

In his polemic *The Cult of the Amateur* Keen (2007) raises some provocative questions regarding the status of the information generated by Web2.0 arguing that what he sees as the destructive force generated by the digital revolution and exercised on our culture, economy and values. It is not democratisation, but is rather a digitalised version of Rousseau's noble savage undermining all that has been achieved by the Enlightenment 'It's ignorance meets egoism meets bad taste meets mob rule … [o]n steroids' (p.1).

Such a position accords well with those who wish to be the guardians of professional knowledge through conventional print media. Seemingly, those who controlled Mode 1 and Mode 2 knowledge through such gatekeeping processes as peer refereeing and publishing contracts would prefer that things remain that way. They seek to privilege the exclusive and excluding realm of academic publishing. The agency of the practitioner is thus limited to being a consumer rather than being engaged in co-construction of professional knowledge.

Insiders and Outsiders

The world of education is a world of many cultures. Those who participate in it may be academics, professional practitioners, students or policy makers. The list is extensive and the needs of each stakeholder complex and nuanced. Understanding these many cultures cannot be obtained from only one source or another. There are two long-standing approaches to apprehending a given culture: the inside perspective that captures the personal beliefs and practices of those who are engaged within it; and, the outside perspective that represents itself as the more objective.

These two views have long been represented in the anthropological literature as the emic and the etic. Emic accounts portray what has taken place in terms of the participants' self-understanding; etic accounts will draw upon comparisons as judged from the outside (Greenfield 1996).

While Mode 1 and Mode 2 knowledge production is clearly that conducted by those who, in the main, stand outside professional practice, Mode 3 Knowledge production opens the gates to those who are both the insiders and outsiders. As Young (2005) so poignantly observes in her account of access to higher education faced by those living and working in economically disadvantaged communities, those closest to the problem rarely have a voice. She argues that there must be means to 'break into the process that (Geertz 1983) identifies whereby academic theories are perpetuated in a closed circle of people who are characters in each other's life stories' (Young 2005:160). Van Galen (2004) goes further in her casti- gation of middle-class academics propensity to speak on behalf of the poor and working class, as well as their willingness to describe and label teachers' work in whatever voice is currently 'in vogue in academic journals' (p.678).

Building professional knowledge, through whichever medium, however, is not only a matter of publication but also one of critique and evaluation – of estimating the error. What are the essential processes for the transformation of information into liberating professional knowledge? We argue that they are related to reflexive thought and the capacity to have courage.

Reflecting and Reflexivity

Much has been written and spoken of in relation to the 'Reflective Practitioner' (Schon 1983) that is one who has a capacity to not only think while engaged in-action, but also reflect on-action itself. It involves acknowledging experience, connecting to prior feelings and attitudes, and making explicit theories-in-use as a means of enhancing understanding and insight.

> The practitioner allows himself [sic] to experience surprise, puzzlement, or confusion in a situation which he finds uncertain or unique. He reflects on the phenomenon before him, and on the prior understandings which have been implicit in his behaviour. He carries out an experiment which serves to generate both a new understanding of the phenomenon and a change in the situation. (Schon 1983: 68)

To be reflective is to have an open mind, to be analytic and deliberative, actively challenging assumptions and epistemologies – or is it? Much of the writing advo- cating teacher reflection assumes that there is a willingness and disposition to engage in this way with professional problems and conundrums. However, even here there is a gap – a gap between what might at worst be a form of 'naval gazing', trapped in taken-for-granted ways of seeing the world, engaging in 'an empty form of defendable compliance' (Power 1999: 42) as outlined in Chapter 1, as opposed to working with peers to unsettle cherished beliefs and hold them up to critical scrutiny. We cannot assume that building professional knowledge, via reflection, will necessarily result in liberation from the constraints of habit, routine and custom especially in these times where work practices have become so intensified. As Lash (2003) has put it:

> We may wish to be reflective but we have neither the time nor space to reflect. We are instead combinards. We put together networks, construct alliances, make deals. We must live, are forced to live, in an atmosphere of risk in which knowledge and life chances are precarious. (pp.51–52)

Even more demanding than being reflective is being reflexive; that is, the capacity not only to reflect upon experiences and circumstances, but also to understand how insight is constructed through socio-historical forces such that the reflection itself is rendered problematic. Three decades ago Giddens (1977) defined reflexivity as 'the rational basis for freedom' (p.28). In other words, to be able to name and locate habits of mind that have accumulated individually, collectively and intergenerationally and which govern responses and professional judgement is liberatory, with the potential to emancipate those who employ its power and force. Just as we have written of Mode 3 knowledge, Giddens (1998) has written of a 'third way' by which the community can re-engage with political life. Reflexivity in this context means the development of new relations of trust and interdependency through processes of dialogue and debate.

Professional knowledge building whereby practitioners can challenge, defend, explicate and question not only the information that comes their way, but also the policies that emerge from it is risky business. If being reflective is a difficult exercise, then being reflexive can be unsettling and discomforting. Many opportunities for teacher professional learning come about through funded projects of one kind or another. Rather than biting the hand that feeds them practitioners are likely to find themselves complicit, unwilling to engage in a critique of underlying policies that generated the projects in the first instance. What is required is the kind of courage discussed in Chapter 3, particularly in its conclusion. We need to continue to ask ourselves what kind of knowledge is required for schools, as organisations, and teachers, as individual practitioners, to engage in authentic participative decision making that also remains provisional and open to reconsideration.

Conclusion

In this sectionwe argue that some of the answers may lie in being defiant. Much has been made, in recent times, of the ways in which teaching requires activism, passion, emotion and care, socially responsible agency and boundless vitality. As we put it in Chapter 3, where are the stories of courage in education? Where is the understanding of education's moral purpose? We suspect that they have not been told, not because they do not exist, but because they are unsung as the knowledge of their existence has not been documented and distributed.

We ask how might we have the collective nerve:

- To agree and take on new ways of working
- To disagree and resist poorly conceived, and often borrowed, rubrics and remedies
- To interrogate the latest fad
- To deal with uncertainty
- To break the mould – to question the orthodoxies that persist, generation after generation
- To return to well-argued, significant theories and reject some of the paralysis of confused contemporary writing
- To regain a comprehensible language in the face of the sludge of the 'bureaucratic-speak' so properly reviled by Don Watson (2003)
- To hold on to serious intellectual ideas
- To treat our teacher education students as learners rather than as clients
- To remember our professional and academic heritage

What we need is the capacity to establish genuine communities of practice based on mutual respect and authentic partnership in order to develop networks of learning as seen by Saunders (2004) to provide valuable space to:

- *Reflect* on practice
- *Reclaim* the language and discourse of pedagogy
- *Relate* professionally with colleagues in schools and universities and collaborate on 'experiments' in teaching and learning
- *Reinforce* the need for an evidence-driven approach to innovation (in the richest sense of the phrase)
- *Restore* a sense of exploration, invention and creativity to classroom planning and practice
- *Create* a more naturally paced, naturally scaled reform, school-led improvement we might say (p.165)

It is clear to us that all of this is possible when new forms of professional knowledge are created and utilised and when the profession equips itself to be defiant (Newman 2006). In this text Newman has challenged activist educators who want to assist people in making up their own minds by understanding how our understanding of practice is informed, negotiated and transacted, and most importantly, interrogated and where appropriate resisted. After all, as we noted earlier in this chapter Lawrence Stenhouse (1979) reminded us that information and knowledge are two different things: 'Information is not knowledge until the factor of error in it is appropriately estimated' (quoted in Stenhouse 1983: 141). Finding the error is, in effect, the act of defiance.

Chapter 5
Inquiry as a Framework for Professional Learning: Interrupting the Dominant Discourse

> *Teachers of today and tomorrow need to do much more learning on the job, or in parallel with it - where they constantly can test out, refine, and get feedback on the improvements they make. They need access to other colleagues in order to learn from them. Schools are poorly designed for integrating learning and teaching on the job. The teaching profession must become a better learning profession.*
>
> (Fullan 2007: 297)

> *[T]he most promising forms of professional development engage teachers in the pursuit of genuine questions, problems, and curiosities, over time, in ways that leave a mark on perspectives, policy, and practice.*
>
> (Warren Little 1993: 133)

The argument that the teaching profession must necessarily become a learning profession is neither new nor revolutionary. Since 1993, when Fullan first pronounced the teaching profession to be not nearly good enough at learning, his work on educational change and leadership has followed this theme (Fullan 1993, 2007), and he is not by any means alone in the call to professional learning action. Furthermore, as Lortie (1975) reminds us, teachers *will* learn as they are socialised into the profession - it is the shape and direction of that learning which, as a profession, we need to be responsible for steering.

It is not entirely the case that compliance is the enemy of authentic learning, but certainly it is possible to see the two concepts as uncomfortable bedfellows. While regimes of compliance privilege the black-and-white over shades of grey, authentic professional learning is an inherently complex business. While it is much easier to measure and quantify the kinds of 'spray on' (Mockler 2005)[1], 'drive by' (Senge et al. 2000) or 'hit and run' (Loucks-Horsley 1999) professional development that are relatively easy to control and 'deliver' to teachers, at the same time questions abound about the effectiveness of such approaches in terms of both teacher learning and impact upon student learning.

---

[1] Initially coined by Serena Veechiet, now ex- director of Teaching and learning, MLC School, Sydney, Australia, in 1998.

S. Groundwater-Smith and N. Mockler, *Teacher Professional Learning in an Age of Compliance*, DOI: 10.1007/978-1-4020-9417-0_5,
© Springer Science+Business Media B.V. 2009

In this chapter, building on the past and future perspectives offered in Chapters 2 and 3, we examine perspectives on professional learning, which both align with and challenge regimes of compliance. We suggest that inquiry can provide a generative framework for teacher professional learning, which responds to Fullan's call for teaching to become a learning profession and meets the short- and long-term needs of teachers and students.

At the outset, it seems that some discussions of the terms 'professional learning' and 'professional development' might be useful, for while the terms are largely used interchangeably in the current age, the movement from 'professional development' to 'professional learning' has been a curious one. Originally construed as a move away from 'one-size-fits-all' in-service style professional development, the movement to adopt the term 'professional learning' within an educational context in the 1990s was linked to the rise of the notion of the 'learning organisation' heralded by the publication of works such as Peter Senge's *The Fifth Discipline* (1992). While 'professional development' was seen as a process whereby teachers passively absorbed information and ideas determined by 'experts' and transmitted via lectures and workshops, 'professional learning' was positioned as a more reflexive, active process in which teachers were engaged in collaboration, self-determination of learning goals and local knowledge creation.

Over the past decade, however, where 'professional learning' has been perceived as the more elegant and innovative of the two, 'professional development' has often become re-badged as 'professional learning' by systems and providers of professional development without great concern for the underlying meaning, to the point where the distinction has become largely a semantic one, more a marker of espoused orientation or intent than anything else.

For us, the difference is much more than semantic. While 'professional development' typically requires little of teachers or facilitators in terms of time, engagement and change, we use 'professional learning' to describe a process, which is highly reflexive and differentiated and which leads to deep pedagogical shifts and transformation of practice. Much of what we see packaged as 'professional learning' is in effect professional development, where teachers are removed from their school context for short periods of time, engage with 'experts' and return to school with little impetus for changed practice. While we do not dispute the significance of this kind of experience in terms of professional networking and opportunities for teachers to connect and talk with colleagues from differing contexts, authentic teacher learning, which leads to improved learning for students is invariably about more than this. We shall discuss what we see as some of the necessary conditions for such learning later in this chapter.

Professional Standards and Professional Development

The drive toward professional standards in education discussed at some length in Chapter 1 has been connected largely to processes of licensing (relating to state control of admission to practice for teachers) and certification (relating to acknowledging and certifying professional accomplishment or leadership) (Darling-Hammond 1999). In some ways, professional standards for teachers can be seen to have emerged from significant challenges in professional learning. (Sachs 2003), for example, discusses the improvement of teachers' performance as one of the driving claims behind the introduction of teaching standards in Australia and in the USA, although as she notes, this argument for professional standards as a catalyst for teacher professional learning 'leaves silent the assumptions about how change will occur and what model of change is implicit' (2003: 180). If this developmental dimension of the current fixation on professional standards is to be taken seriously, then the potential for authentic professional learning they afford must necessarily be valued also.

In outlining what she regards as the recent confluence of teaching quality and teacher accountability, in the context of regimes of standards and compliance, Marilyn Cochran-Smith writes:

> Policies intended to improve teaching quality can only be as good as the underlying conceptions of teaching, learning, and schooling on which they are based. Unfortunately, as a number of critics (including myself) have argued (Cochran-Smith 2001; Earley 2000; Engel 2000), many current policies and policy recommendations share narrow - and some would say impoverished - notions of teaching and learning that do not account for the complexities that are at the heart of the educational enterprise in a democratic society. (Cochran-Smith 2003: 3)

Similarly, as a strategy for teacher professional learning leading to improved teaching and learning, professional standards can only be as good as the processes they employ. Hand in hand with the proliferation of professional standards and teacher accreditation in education has come the requirement that teachers undertake a stipulated amount of professional development in order to maintain accreditation. The implicit privileging of 'professional development' approaches to teacher professional learning, approaches which are widely recognised to have little impact or effect upon changed classroom practice and improved teaching and learning (Garet et al. 2001) means that while in this endeavour that which passes for 'professional learning' can be neatly quantified and 'ticked off' as per the requirements of the culture of compliance, very little real professional learning need necessarily have taken place. The emperor can thus proudly march on while audit society pundits congratulate him loudly upon his splendid new clothes.

While the continuing professional development dimension of accreditation by the National Board for Professional Teaching Standards in the USA and the Teacher Development Agency for Schools in the UK is more expansive and does emphasise the range of different experiences that might go toward significant professional learning for accomplished teachers (including that, which is inquiry-based), in Australia an orientation toward a 'professional development' model is evident. Teacher accreditation in Australia is the province of the various accreditation bodies within Australian states (e.g. the Queensland College of Teachers, New South Wales Institute of Teachers and Victorian Institute for Teachers), which have been established over the past 5 years. In New South Wales, once accredited, teachers must complete professional development, quantified in hours, to retain accreditation at the level of professional competence: 50 h of 'Institute Registered' professional development and 50 h of 'Teacher Identified' professional development. Institute-registered professional development is provided by accredited continuing education providers and organised into 'courses' and 'programmes' (which comprise a series of courses).

In Victoria, the situation is similar, with teachers required to undertake 100 h of continuing professional development, interestingly referred to as 'professional learning' on the navigation tool of the Institute's web site, despite the documentation discussing 'professional development' exclusively. Half of these 'activities' must provide access to research and knowledge sourced from outside the school, while the other may be activities identified by teachers as contributing to their professional growth and development. In Fig. 5.1, the VIT professional development activities record is notable both for its conceptualisation of professional learning as a series of 'activities' and as its implicit assumption that an 'external presenter or a colleague' presenting new knowledge adds value to the process.

The problem with such a conceptualisation of teacher professional learning is manifold. First, it is located firmly within an outdated industrial model of education, which takes the transmission of knowledge as given. Second, it equates learning with hours spent 'on task', rather than focusing upon improved understanding, changed practice, effect upon student learning or any other indicator of professional

PROFESSIONAL DEVELOPMENT ACTIVITIES RECORD   teaching

TEACHER'S NAME:						REGISTRATION NUMBER:		
List the professional development activities you have undertaken.	Describe the nature of the professional activities you have undertaken by ticking the appropriate columns						Activities providing access to research and knowledge sourced from outside the school environment	Hours
All activities should relate to the standards of professional practice	Within the school with an external presenter or a colleague presenting new knowledge	Within the school in collaboration with other colleagues	External to the school	Undertaken on the initiative of the teacher, either in or out of school	Other (Provide details)			
Date	Activity							

Teachers are required to undertake at least 100 hours of professional development activities in the five years leading up to their due date for renewal of registration.
All activities must have a reference to the standards of professional practice.
At least half the activities must provide access to research and knowledge sourced from outside the immediate school or work environment.
The balance of activities can come from either more activities providing access to research and knowledge sourced from outside the immediate school environment or activities teachers identify as contributing to their professional practice, knowledge or well-being.

Fig. 5.1 Victorian Institute of Teachers Professional Development Activities Record (VIT 2008)

learning. Third, linked to this, it measures what is readily measurable (i.e. hours) rather than those elements which are more ephemeral and difficult to compare between teachers. Fourth, it conceptualises teacher professional learning as a series of discrete 'activities' or 'episodes' rather than as the ongoing process that effective teacher professional learning is known to be (Loucks-Horsley 1999). Fifth, in privileging the 'outside' developed professional learning over that which is 'teacher identified' - in the case of both NSW and Victoria it is mandated that at least 50 of the 100 h is to be the former, if not more - teachers' professional learning agenda is effectively determined by external providers, and thus cannot but be episodic and disjointed in nature.

We are not claiming here that professional teaching standards run counter to a transformative inquiry-based approach to professional learning, although it seems to be the case that in the two Australian examples considered here, the opportunity presented to take advantage of a more creative and contemporary model of professional learning on a state-wide basis has been overlooked.

Professional teaching standards do not alone and will not ever improve the quality of teaching and learning. Much as a rubric developed to assess student performance on a task is effective not because it captures in a watertight manner what student performance will 'look like' at various levels of achievement, but rather because it provides a starting point for *making assessment explicit and transparent*, so too it is with professional teaching standards. The standards themselves provide a starting point for discussion of what accomplished professional practice 'looks like': descriptive as standards may be, they do not at face value convey a quantifiable, replicateable 'essence of teacher'. Their power is not in the words and sentences they contain, but rather in the scope they offer to build a shared understanding of what it is that an accomplished teacher knows and does, and in the processes that sit behind the expression of accomplishment, representing the opening of professional practice to debate, discussion and improvement.

Professional Standards, 'Evidence' and the Review of Professional Practice

If professional standards in education hold any promise for improving the quality of teaching and learning, then it is through their capacity to foster generative and authentic professional learning that this promise will come to fruition. The capacity of any system of accreditation or review in this area lies not in the 'quality assurance' implicit in quantifying the professional development 'hours' required to be undertaken by accomplished teachers in any period of time, but rather in the *processes* the system utilises for review and accreditation of professional practice. Unfortunately, in most instances where professional standards are being utilised, this opportunity for standards to be a catalyst for authentic professional learning is not being realised in favour of a compliance and accountability approach driven by an administrative rather than developmental imperative.

In her dual focus on the relentless complexity of teachers' work and the power of inquiry as a tool for teacher development and renewal, Cochran-Smith's work provides some clues into what this potential might be and how it might (or might not) be realised. Her more recent work presents a warning to educators in times of accountability and compliance that while simple answers (and processes such as these) might go a way toward addressing complex questions, they seldom provide adequate or long-term solutions:

> *Teaching is unforgivingly complex.* It is not simply good or bad, right or wrong, working or failing. Although absolutes and dichotomies such as these are popular in the headlines and in campaign slogans, they are limited in their usefulness...They ignore almost completely the nuances of 'good' (or 'bad') teaching of real students collected in actual classrooms in the context of particular times and places. They mistake reductionism for clarity, myopia for insight. (Cochran-Smith 2003: 4, emphasis in original)

Issues of teacher quality and accountability have taken centre stage in public debate about education across the UK, the USA and Australia (as elsewhere in the western world) over the past decade. Linked to the growing focus in the same time frame on professional standards, many attempts to quantify and measure teachers' professional practice have fallen into the trap of privileging the easy to measure but trivial over the difficult to measure but important (Darling-Hammond 1996). The assessment of teachers' work is made more difficult by the truth behind David Labaree's observation (2000) that teaching is an enormously difficult job that looks easy.

This is not to argue, however, against accountability on the part of the teaching profession. Teachers need to be accountable - primarily to their students, but also to their schools, colleagues and society more broadly - for what they do and how they do it. In his meta-analysis of research on influences on student achievement, John Hattie found that 'what teachers know, do and care about' (Hattie 2003: 2) is responsible for approximately 30% of variance in student achievement, representing the greatest source of variance after students themselves. This assessment is supported in the work of US educator Linda Darling-Hammond, who writes 'when all is said and done, what matters most for students' learning are the commitments and capacities of their teachers' (Darling-Hammond 1997: 293). She continues, however, to suggest some implications of this for schools and school systems:

> Teaching for understanding cannot be produced solely by spending more money or by requiring that schools use specific texts or curriculum packages, and it cannot be driven by mandating new tests, even better ones. Although things like standards, funding and management are essential supports, the *sine qua non* of education is whether teachers know how to make complex subjects accessible to diverse learners and whether they can work in partnership with parents and other educators to support children's development. If only a few teachers have this capacity, most schools will never be able to produce better education for the students who attend them. Wide-spread success depends in the development of a professionwide base of knowledge along with a commitment to the success of all students. (1997: 293–294)

This focus upon teaching and 'teacher quality' as the keystone of student achievement suggests that the evaluation and improvement of professional practice is an important part of improving student learning outcomes. Furthermore, the links between effective teacher professional learning and improvement of professional practice and student learning outcomes are well documented in the research literature (see, e.g. Borko 2004). Together, these two observations lend weight to the argument that processes and practices which make use of professional standards for purposes of accreditation or acknowledgement of professional accomplishment that feed into and generate professional development and learning are required, and further that they should actively seek to build on what we know about the kinds of professional learning that makes a difference to teachers and students.

In order for these generative outcomes to be achieved, the structures and processes through which professional practice is reviewed and reflected upon need to be linked to a clearly defined and communicated purpose behind the process. Figure 5.2 represents a heuristic for understanding different models of reviewing professional practice, linked to the purpose of the exercise (represented on the horizontal axis) and the location of power within the exercise (represented on the vertical axis). Our observation is that most exercises which aim to in some way review, evaluate or assess teachers' professional practice fall into one of the four quadrants represented in Fig. 5.2. Each of the two axes is intended to represent a continuum upon which purpose and power might be 'plotted', rather than a pair of absolutes representing a bipolar dichotomy - it is rarely the case that either purpose or power is located at the very end of the scale.

These four quadrants give rise to four separate ways of thinking about reviewing professional practice, and we shall briefly discuss each of these here.

Quadrant 1: Review as Compliance

Reviews of practice situated within quadrant 1 are predominantly designed as a tool by which the system or school's leadership team, executive or principal can ensure compliance with the school's goals or mission via surveillance or 'inspection' of teachers, yet one in which teachers have a level of agency or decision-making

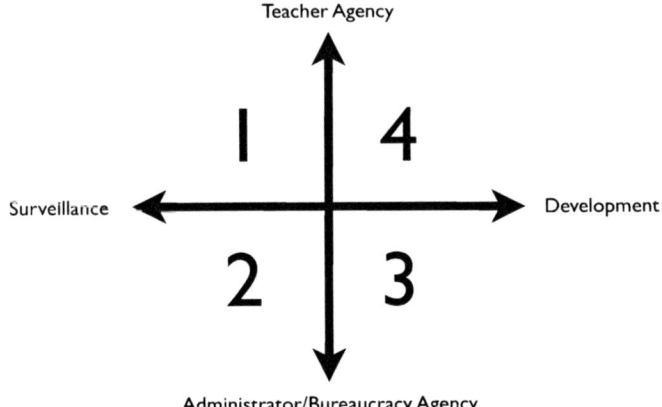

Fig. 5.2 A heuristic for considering review of teachers' professional practice

power. Approaches that fall into this quadrant might have a structure and approach determined by the school, but a capacity for teachers to determine what the particular focus of the review will be and/or the ways in which evidence might be gathered and used. Quadrant 1 processes generally utilise school hierarchical structures (where teachers are 'reviewed by' their Head of Department or Faculty, Heads of Department are 'reviewed by' the Director of Studies/Deputy Principal and so on). The processes used in accreditation of teachers at the level of Professional Competence by the NSW Institute of Teachers is, in its intent,[2] located within this quadrant: within the process, beginning teachers are accorded agency in the collection, annotation and presentation of evidence for accreditation, while the key goal of the exercise is to ensure teacher quality and compliance with minimum standards of competence.

Quadrant 2: Review as Performance Management

Teacher review situated within quadrant 2 has an intent or purpose reaching toward inspection or surveillance, similar to that described above, while the bulk of power within the process is held by the bureaucracy or school administration. Within this quadrant, the process is presented as 'one-size-fits-all', which teachers generally experience as something to be 'done to' them. This approach largely assumes a 'deficit' between expectations and teacher performance, and while it certainly allows for management of teacher performance where concerns or performance issues have arisen in relation to a particular teacher, as a whole-school approach it is more likely to induce mistrust and competition between teachers than foster the kind of generative professional learning environment within which both teachers and students can be expected to flourish. While performance management is an important aspect of the role of school leaders as part of their responsibility to students and the school community, as an approach to professional review for all teachers this model fails to seize the potential of the process and may in fact be detrimental to the fabric of the learning community.

Quadrant 3: Review as Professional Development

Teacher review situated within quadrant 3 takes the same 'one-size-fits-all' approach characteristic of quadrant 2, where the power within the process resides predominantly with administrators or bureaucrats, while the purpose and intent of

---

[2] We choose to qualify this observation by stating that the process is 'in its intent' located within quadrant 1: the enactment of the process is to some extent overseen by schools and systems, and via some of the processes put into place by Teacher Accreditation Authorities in different locations, beginning teachers have been accorded less agency in the process than the Institute originally intended.

the process is predominantly developmental. Processes used for recognition of professional excellence, such as those employed in the NSW Quality Teaching Awards (Australian College of Educators 2008), and in the accreditation of teachers at levels of *Experienced Teacher* and *Classroom/Professional Excellence* within the Independent Schools sector in NSW (Independent Schools Teacher Accreditation Authority 2008a, b) are located within this quadrant. Within these processes, teachers have limited agency (e.g. the key decision to engage in the process resides with teachers themselves), while in the interests of cross-system comparison and compliance, the bulk of the 'power' within the process resides outside the school, within the accrediting organisation.

Quadrant 4: Review as Teacher Formation and Renewal

Review processes within quadrant 4 take teacher development as their key purpose and require the power within the process to be genuinely shared by the school/system and teacher. To this end, key decisions about how and where evidence will be collected and what the focus of the review will be might be established by the teacher in consultation with colleagues. The process might also be seen as a cyclical one, where the collection and analysis of evidence gives way at the conclusion of the process to new approaches and practices, which themselves might become subject to the next 'phase' of review. Approaches that enact a practitioner-inquiry or evidenced-based practice approach are generally located within this quadrant, and are constructed such that they lead to outcomes which foster a generative and healthy learning culture within the school.

We offer these insights into the approaches that might be taken in the review and evaluation of teachers' professional practice not because we believe that such processes need necessarily form the basis of an inquiry-based professional learning model, but rather because, as a driving agenda within educational practice in the current age, it is salient to note that such processes, however they are *generally* enacted within schools and systems, need not *necessarily* be geared towards compliance. Indeed, processes of review and evaluation are not mutually exclusive in their aims from those of effective and authentic professional learning, and it is to the tenets of these that we now turn.

Teacher Professional Learning in an Age of Compliance

Over 20 years ago Susan Loucks-Horsley and colleagues (Loucks-Horsley et al. 1987: 8) outlined ten characteristics of successful teacher development programmes, these being the following:

- Collegiality and collaboration
- Experimentation and risk-taking
- Incorporation of available knowledge bases
- Appropriate participant involvement in goal setting, implementation, evaluation and decision making
- Time to work on staff development and assimilate new learnings
- Leadership and sustained administrative support
- Appropriate incentives and rewards
- Designs built on principles of adult learning and the change process
- Integration of individual goals with school goals
- Formal placement of the programme within the philosophy and organisational structure of the school

To these, we suggested some years ago adding 'a culture of enquiry within schools', suggesting that such a culture both reflects and fosters authentic professional learning (Groundwater-Smith and Mockler 2003a).

While these characteristics are somewhat aged, we also find that they were in fact ahead of their time, and that few of them have been realised in most contexts, on either a school or systemic level. In addition, regimes of compliance and accountability have seen a number of these characteristics come under threat, as they have become increasingly countercultural in the context of dominant discourses surrounding education. Collegiality and collaboration, for example, defined by Loucks-Horsley et al. as that which 'is more than congeniality; it means connecting on a professional level with other school staff, looking for new ideas, advice, a forum to test models of teaching' (1987: 8) is under threat from approaches and processes which heighten and indeed privilege individualism. The very idea of experimentation and risk-taking in education runs counter to compliance in its purist form, which aims to quantify and document acceptable practices and processes, and, as suggested above, the capacity for teachers to have power and agency in determining the professional learning goals is often limited by the ways in which processes of review and 'audit' are implemented.

We believe, however, that while these characteristics are still yet to be realised in most contexts that they do not stand opposed to notions of quality and accountability, but rather that it is possible to see compliance with these notions as the 'base line' or lowest common denominator, where authentic and effective professional learning can be built upon a foundation of accountability and quality that moves beyond and indeed quite surpasses 'compliance'. For us, the central tenet of such a professional learning approach takes a collaborative and inquiry-based focus, which both meets and yet challenges the requirements of the compliance culture. Sachs (2007) suggests that such an approach can be conceptualised as professional learning as 're-imagining', a form of professional learning, which 'is highly political and serves to advocate and support change from a variety of perspectives and approaches' (p.7). In this it contrasts starkly with views of professional learning that focus upon 'retooling', 'remodelling' or 'revitalising' the profession.

Conclusion: Towards an Inquiry-Based Model of Professional Learning

Over the past decade, (Cochran-Smith and Lytle 1999, 2007) have developed the notion 'inquiry as stance' as an organising construct for teacher learning, both pre-service and in-service.

> Inquiry as stance is distinct from the more common notion of inquiry as time-bounded project or discrete activity within a teacher education course or professional development workshop. Teachers and student teachers who take an inquiry stance work within inquiry communities to generate local knowledge, envision and theorize their practice, and interpret and interrogate the theory and research of others. (1999: 289)

Based upon ideas about professional knowledge and knowledge construction congruent with those outlined in Chapters 4, inquiry as stance, then, is an orientation on the part of teachers toward generation of and engagement with their own curiosities about their work, ongoing grappling with critical questions they confront in their classrooms, and a willingness to engage in debates about practice both within and beyond the school. Such an orientation brings to life Lieberman and Miller's vision of professional learning:

> Teaching and learning are interdependent, not separate functions. In this view, teachers are primarily learners. They are problem posers and problem solvers; they are researchers; and they are intellectuals engaged in unraveling the learning process both for themselves and for the young people in their charge. Learning is not consumption; it is knowledge production. (Lieberman and Miller 1990: 112)

An inquiry-based model of professional learning privileges knowledge production over knowledge consumption; the posing of questions over the development of watertight answers; the generation of curiosity and debate over the inclination to settle easily upon a position. It responds to the call of Judith Warren Little in the opening quotation of this chapter to have teachers' knowledge and learning contribute to changing policy and practice. It requires the 'local' and expert knowledge held by teachers to be utilised and sat beside (and at times butted up against) knowledge generated outside the school and outside the profession, in ways such as those suggested in Chapters 4. It requires a willingness to collaborate and forge true collegiality which brings teachers into professional discourse with each other about things that really matter for their schools, their students and society more broadly. And it requires a willingness to navigate the unsettling, the uncomfortable and sometimes the downright messy in the negotiation of professional learning that meets the needs of teachers and their students and schools, on the part of schools and teachers themselves, as well as those of us who work alongside teachers in the interests of professional learning.

Chapter 6
Reclaiming Quality

> *It is clear that we live in a world full of quality companies, following quality practices, winning quality awards. Despite this, unfortunately, words such as trust, integrity and virtue still fail to hold significant meaning. … Whilst we have put labels of so called 'excellence' on virtually every motif of modern existence, we need only glance around to note the reality. In modern society, we have lost the skill to pay attention to things that are noble. The truth is that, despite the rhetoric, we have increasingly come to judge merit and value by external veneer rather than inner worth.*
>
> (Ahmed and Machold 2004: 527–528)

While Ahmed and Machold write here of the commercial world, there can be no question that the rhetoric of 'quality' and 'total quality management' has pervaded educational practices at both the local and wider levels. The word 'quality' has drummed itself into the consciousness of consumers, whether they be consumers of goods or of services such as schooling. A flurry of announcements, pronouncements, programmes, projects and publications cry out 'quality' regardless of how well the enterprise is being undertaken. School billboards declare that they are offering a quality education to their students; education systems assert that they are in pursuit of quality teaching and learning. But what does it all mean? We suspect that much of it is a case of smoke and mirrors, in the hands of clever spin doctors. It is for this reason that this chapter seeks to reclaim issues surrounding quality. Thus, we shall discuss some new dimensions of quality, particularly as they relate to ethical practices and virtue, and we shall investigate ways in which quality as a trivial concept can be transcended and reincorporated into a wider and richer vision of informed practice. In the latter part of the chapter, we shall also consider quality within a broader discussion of accountability and responsibility. We shall draw the argument together by citing a case of teacher inquiry in a context where there are dilemmas and contradictions in meeting accountability requirements and professional responsibility maxims that we characterise as moral responsibility.

S. Groundwater-Smith and N. Mockler, *Teacher Professional Learning in an Age of Compliance*, DOI: 10.1007/978-1-4020-9417-0_6,
© Springer Science + Business Media B.V. 2009

New Dimensions of Quality

A groundbreaking project with respect to quality in what they have called 'applied and practice-based research in education' was undertaken by Furlong and Oancea in 2006 and reported in their 2008 publication. They enjoined their readers to engage critically with the view of 'quality' that they had embraced, this being *excellence or virtue* in a classical (Aristotelian) sense of the terms' (p.3) They argued that their definition of quality far exceeded the scientific, impact and productivity indicators for quality, hitherto used as criteria by various funding bodies in the UK. In order to assess quality within this definition they looked for the constituents of excellence in applied and practice-based research and the relationships between them; they called these the following 'domains':

> *The epistemic domain* embracing trustworthiness, the contribution to knowledge, transparency and explicitness in design and reporting, and paradigm-dependent consideration
>
> *The technical domain* including fitness to purpose, specificity, concern for enabling impact, operationalizability, propriety, and strategic and economic value
>
> *The phronetic domain* relating to transformation, deliberation, reflexivity and criticism, engagement, plausibility, salience and timeliness, receptiveness and dialogue (Furlong and Oancea 2008: 10–14)

This synthesis barely covers the complex arguments produced by Furlong and Oancea which were then the subject of a series of responses, and also included in their book. Among these was our own contribution (Groundwater-Smith and Mockler 2008) where we argue that the overriding criterion governing quality in practitioner inquiry should be a consideration of an ethical stance.

It is our contention that if attention is not explicitly paid to being ethical in professional practice, then what follows will always be subject to questioning. Having an Aristotelian consciousness as required by Furlong and Oancea allows us to examine the matter of quality through a critical lens. In particular, in the context of this book, we have an interest in the quality of teacher professional learning that is informed by methodologically principled inquiry that permits dialogue and debate, and that admits to the problematics of practice. Too often, it would seem that a pragmatic solution is what is sought, rather than a better understanding of the problem. Instead of seeking to understand *how* the educational world unfolds, the pressure is towards unfolding the educational world to fit the needs and demands of educational employing authorities. As we have argued at some length in Chapter 2, too often administrators and professional development specialists see teacher inquiry as the new 'silver bullet' that they wish to control and domesticate.

An important corrective to the control of practitioner inquiry, as an *end* in itself, is to work in the direction of the *means*, that is, the manner in which the inquiry is undertaken. A number of programmes in a variety of countries have now turned to developing a more fruitful relationship between field-based practitioners and their academic counterparts such that they work in a partnership with one another with the shared intention of improving the quality of practice. By engaging in reciprocal and respectful dialogue across the sectors there is much to be learned about practice. Cochran-Smith and Lytle (2007) consider such collective enterprises as 'working the dialectic' (p.31). By this they argue that it is possible to conceptualise, undertake, analyse and theorise inquiry in ways that can assist its development into forms of public knowledge about practice because it is a multi-vocal endeavour embracing a wide range of sometimes competing perspectives. They are enthusiastic about the idea of inquiry as a 'pedagogy of teacher education' (p.35), a concept that is embraced in this book. Importantly, they argue for the benefits that come from the messiness of combining these worlds. Putting quality and messiness together is a challenge for us all and certainly adds a new dimension to the debate in which quality has often been trivialised.

Transcending the Trivial

Clearly, for us, recognising the relationship between quality and ethics is no trivial consideration. As Hazlett, McAdam and Murray (2007) assert 'quality lives in symbiosis with ethics' (p.671). As we have argued, ethical practice is the essential foundation upon which authentic quality enterprises are built.

In their account of the connection between quality and ethics, Ahmed and Machold (2004) provide us with another set of domains for ethical accountability, as a form of moral responsibility, voiced as maxims, these being:

- The Maxim of No-harm
- The Maxim of Transparency
- The Maxim of Voice
- The Maxim of Equity
- The Maxim of Benefit
- The Maxim of Integrity
- The Maxim of Liberty
- The Maxim of Care (pp.539–542)

These ethical frameworks of awareness have much to say to us as practitioner researchers intent upon improving the conditions of the many aspects of schooling. While they have been constructed within a discourse of business practices we wish to elaborate them within a context of professional learning.

The Maxim of No-Harm

Here we need to ask ourselves whether the inquiry and its processes have been 'safe' for all who have been involved. We cannot unequivocally promise to do no harm, because we cannot always anticipate the effects of our investigations; what we can do is ensure that we minimise harm. This is best illustrated by an example.

One of us worked with parents in focus group discussions in a large independent girls school. Parents reflected upon their own learning experiences, what had helped and assisted them and how effective their learning had been. They then turned to the experiences of their daughters and considered their school learning. Mindful of having a membership check of the account of the focus group discussion the parents were asked to respond to an email that portrayed the focus group in a draft form. It would, once cleared, be made available for the public record. One parent printed out the draft and circulated it in the school playground much to the chagrin of others who had some corrections to make. On reflection it would have been important to caution the parents about the confidential nature of the draft before sending it to them. This may seem a minor transgression; however, it is illustrative of the ways in which potential harm might be minimised.

The Maxim of Transparency

In our view covert research is not only unethical, but also questionable. After all, if the inquirer is covering up what she or he is doing how can it be validated? Some arguments have been made to allow forms of 'hearsay' into an inquiry - what is heard in the playground, for example. Fine (1992) provides a poignant account of a conversation between herself as a volunteer rape counsellor and an emergency room patient. No informed consent was obtained because the encounter was not anticipated. The researcher in this case had not set out to disguise her intention, as she felt that in developing an account of the encounter she was not harming the subject because publication would be far removed and the case anonymised. What kinds of checks and balances do we have here? We would argue that the publication of the anecdote, while being illuminative, is also exploitative, especially of someone in a vulnerable situation. Furthermore, this story in itself highlights one of the difficulties of conducting research in one's own backyard, as it were, for as one of us has pointed out elsewhere, the stories generated even in the context of our own professional practice are not always ours to tell (Mockler 2007).

The Maxim of Voice

In ethical accountability it is of significance that the voices of the range of stakeholders are attended to. In Chapter 7, where we address what is at stake and what is at risk, we discuss the matter of making students' voices audible, for they are the consequential stakeholders with respect to decisions that are made about schooling practices. Anna Clark in her account of Australian secondary school children's views of learning history points out that in the robust and sometimes acrimonious debate about the place and nature of history in the school curriculum the students themselves are rarely consulted. As she put it: 'It is all too easy to think students don't know what's good for them; they hate school anyway, so why ask them how they learn. They think Australian history's boring, so why bother getting their opinions on the subject?' (2008: 141). Of course it is not only students who deserve to be listened to, although they are usually the last to be consulted; it is also important to take into account the views of the many contributors to the education enterprise including professional staff, ancillary staff and parents themselves.

The Maxim of Equity

When a range of stakeholders is being consulted, as argued above, it is also important to ensure that they are treated with equal consideration and respect. Too often the least powerful are marginalised at worst and patronised at best.

The Maxim of Benefit

This principle derives from the need to examine the benefits of a particular inquiry. Who gains, who loses? For example, if a school's professional learning team is investigating the provision of resources for gifted and talented students are they also taking into account the costs in terms of the needs of those who may be struggling? Are the gains made at the expense of the learning of others? Is the trade-off worth it? How long- or short-term are the benefits likely to be? Such questions can be often neglected in the pursuit of quality for some and not for others. This is a highly salient problem when we turn to our discussion of accountabilities later in this chapter.

The Maxim of Integrity

Here we need to ask ourselves whether the environment is one that encourages and makes explicit ethical behaviour. If we are consulting students are they aware of the purposes of our investigation? Are there conditions of mutual trust and respect? Will the resulting professional practices lead to better conditions for learning?

The Maxim of Liberty

Schooling, in many ways, is a coercive enterprise. Most children in the developed world have no choice in whether they will be in school or not. There is a potential spillover into their right to participate in teacher inquiry intended to contribute to teacher professional learning. Generally, informed consent is obtained from parents, but rarely is it obtained from the students themselves. When their work is being examined as evidence of learning outcomes, when they are mass tested, when they are interviewed, when they are observed in the classroom or the playground, are they advised of the purposes to which the data will be put? At the same time, examination of student work to determine the achievement of learning outcomes is a core component of the teaching and learning process itself, and this is in some ways demonstrative of the often blurred lines between practitioner research and practice itself.

In another sense it can also be argued that the professional liberty of teachers themselves is also being pressed upon. As national government increases, their hold on curriculum, assessment and various aspects of teacher education, matters of professional autonomy and the right to question policies and practices are increasingly impinged upon. This matter is discussed in Chapter 7 as it was in Chapter 2, but if quality in education is to be a goal, then having opportunities to examine underlying moral principles is an essential component of that goal. As Freiesleben and Pohl (2004) put it:

> As quality professionals, we may perceive morals as a mere playing field for moralists or philosophers, being far detached from the 'real' world we deal with and having nothing to contribute to solving our problems. By doing so, we neglect something important. Morals are at the heart of human cooperation and therefore also important for the process of improving quality. (p.1210)[1]

The Maxim of Care

Many of these issues have already been flagged, but are worth considering once more; they closely relate to matters of rights, responsibilities and communitarian well-being and again are the sources of a number of questions. Are the rights of some given less consideration than the rights of others? Is cooperation actively rather than passively sought? Are matters of discontent and disassociation addressed? Is positive and insightful behaviour acknowledged and nurtured?

If we are ethically and socially responsible, it means that we are concerned with both purposes and practices. Kemmis (2007) believes that much that passes for participatory inquiry in education is more concerned with the latter than the former. So that an emphasis is given to improving techniques of teaching as opposed to examining the broader questions around schooling, the efficiency of practices is

---

[1] It may have been noted that many of the references for this chapter do not come from the education literature but from the writings of those associated with quality management. This is not by chance. We believe that as education has increasingly drawn upon the management field it is important not only to perceive it as informing strategic management, but also as a source for considering larger ethical and moral questions. After all, Adam Smith, as long ago as 1759 in his work *Theory of Moral Sentiments,* made it clear that virtue, self-regulation and sympathy are important and inescapable capacities for human enterprises of every kind.

examined to the exclusion of evaluating the social, cultural, discursive and material-economic consequences of those practices. He sees that the goal is conformity in terms of the agenda of government with little recourse to examining alternative perspectives. Furthermore, Kemmis raises the important issue of developing inter-subjective understanding by engaging in critique in an environment where all voices might be heard. He concludes his argument by turning to those matters of quality with which this chapter is so concerned:

> [T]he quality of practitioner research is not just a matter of the technical excellence of practitioner research as 'research'. It is a matter of addressing important problems in thought and action, in theory and practice - problems worth addressing in and for our times, in and for our communities, in and for our shared world. It is a matter of addressing important problems for education, for the good of each person, and for the good of our societies. (p.21)

In more closely addressing important problems for education we would argue that there is also a case for considering the matters of accountability and responsibility and the ways in which they might be aligned with the quality of practice.

Accountability, Responsibility and Quality

While accountability and responsibility appear to go hand in hand, in fact the relationship between the two is highly problematic when placed together in a discourse of quality.

Many years ago one of us wrote:

> A recent television commercial showed an exultant mother demonstrating a domestic product to her teacher-daughter, underlining her successful use of the product with the words, 'Results Jan, isn't that what a teacher wants?' What does a teacher want? What is wanted of a teacher? (Groundwater-Smith and Nicoll 1980: 123)

Clearly the implication is that what is wanted of a teacher and indeed of an education system is 'results'. The teacher and system are accountable to the students and their parents for obtaining positive outcomes that will lead young people to become productive, self-actualised and well-rounded citizens.

Results, though, can mean very different things to those who have a stake in education: students, parents, employers unions, government and the broader community. While being responsible for accountability, is it also the case that accountability should be responsibly enacted? To unravel this complicated knitting together of ideas we turn first to the ways that accountability is understood and undertaken in school education.

Accountability: The 'Elephant in the Room'

The phrase 'the elephant in the room' has come to connote something obvious, which nonetheless is overlooked or goes unaddressed, or where there is a reluctance to confront a given and significant problem. As we argued in Chapter 1 in relation to the audit society, accountability in education is burgeoning in every developed country, irrespective of the shade of government. It is to be found most notably in the No Child Left Behind (NCLB) legislation in the USA, under a conservative regime but equally exists in the UK, principally England, under New Labour, which has built on the former Thatcher government's neo-liberal policies. It is present in every Australian state and territory at both federal and state levels and is to be found in a range of European contexts. So what is it and how has it come to be so prominent, yet rarely discussed when matters of teacher professional learning arise? Is it the 'elephant in the room'?

In essence, accountability is tied to established norms and practices in relation to efficient and effective use of resources, whether financial, material or human. The process considers whether the services to which the resources are to be put have produced the desired results with commensurate rewards and consequences. In other words, are the investments in education paying off?

It is worth looking more closely at the NCLB Act and its impact in terms of accountability because it is such a significant case. As Hollingsworth and Gallego (2007) put it:

> In 2001, Congress passed the No Child Left Behind Act, a new twist on the Elementary and Secondary Education Act. It signalled a sea change in federal education policy as it moved beyond 'compliance' with the former elementary and secondary education law to demonstrated accountability via large-scale standardized test results and the disaggregation of data by specific subgroups. (p.454)

The NCLB Act was launched in the USA as a bipartisan policy to address lagging literacy standards and the growing achievement gap between students from diverse backgrounds. With the most notable accountability measure being standardised testing a number of issues came to the fore. Important among these is whether such testing fosters or undermines academic standards, whether, in effect, the desired quality is being achieved. McNeil (2002) in making this point also argues that an unintended effect of the dominance of high-stakes standardised tests 'is to shift the locus of control of school policies and practices away from teachers, parents and communities and into an expert domain whose vocabulary is at a far remove' (p.244), the experts being the test designers. Thus, those closest to the students, the teachers, are accountable for the ends but not the means.

As we noted in Chapter 1, the rhetoric of NCLB is hard to contest. It is an argument for more equal outcomes from schooling to be achieved, irrespective of race, ethnicity, gender or social class. As Linda Darling Hammond (2006) has pointed out international assessments reveal that America's schools are 'among the most unequal in the industrialised world in terms of spending, curriculum offerings, teaching quality and outcomes' (p.13). However, the practical outcomes look a little different when the mechanisms for making schools and teachers accountable are, to say the least, heavy-handed and coercive. Compliance in relation to the teaching methods to be adopted and the testing measures to record outcomes is controlled through sanctions and incentives provided for districts, schools and teachers.

In line with our earlier discussion of quality and ethics it can be posited that coercion is unlikely to produce deep and profound changes in practice. Bryk and Schneider (2002) in their landmark study of Chicago Schools make the case that schools with a high degree of relational trust are far more likely to enhance student achievement than those where social relations are poor. They ask four key questions: Do all participants in the school environment respect each other and each other's ideas? Do they believe in one another's competence, abilities and potential? Do they have a personal regard for each other? And, will they act with integrity when it comes to the interests of the students? These qualities are seen to be far more likely to contribute to school reform than the crude accountability mechanisms inherent in NCLB.

Of course the USA is not alone in its marrying of high-stakes testing to accountability with some highly problematic results. The creation of school 'league tables' in the UK was seen by its protagonists to be a form of leverage that would drive underperforming schools to develop procedures and practices that would make them attractive to parents and their children. Schools would be accountable for their results, especially at the later secondary level. The comparison between schools was made possible by the development of a national curriculum and a national testing regime that would cover the designated key stages. Many studies have addressed the problematics of a process whereby a school is positioned on the league table in relation to General Certificate of School Education (GCSE) results. Schools are judged on the percentage of students who achieve at least five GCSE grades at A to C. In a study that revealed the hidden costs of league tables Gillborn and Youdell (2000) demonstrated that African Caribbean students and their working class white peers were disadvantaged in that their learning counted for little in the process. Schools are separating out those who will achieve in the top bands and providing additional coaching for those who bridge the D to C divide. *The Guardian* newspaper (Berliner 2002) reports Ted Wragg, respected Professor of Education at Exeter University, as saying:

> A lot of effort goes into those at the D/C borderline. The schools who don't do it are regarded as the dozy ones. It is purely to massage their position in the league tables. All forms of league tables are misleading and the five A to C measure has a malign influence on what goes on in schools.

In the same article David Gillborn likens school practices to a kind of medical triage on the battlefield where doctors with finite resources assess the wounded to see who should be treated first. Being well positioned on the league tables is a matter of survival. Markets and competition are seen to create economies of student worth in which students are deemed to be worthy, or not, on the basis of whether they are an asset or liability in relation to the performance benchmarks to which schools must aspire.

In such local economies of student worth those young people who are seen as having high levels of academic potential and as being manageable and teachable are highly valued and sought after by schools. Conversely, those students who are perceived as being of lower academic 'ability', or those having special needs, or present behavioural challenges, or who are recent immigrants who may be traumatised and/

or have additional language needs are actively discouraged from enrolling. The question becomes 'to whom are the schools accountable?' To the parents who are seeking to establish some kind of quasi-selectivity, perhaps yearning for the days before comprehensive education? Or, to the young people who are struggling to learn and need support and assistance. And, what kind of quality is being offered here?

It is evident from both the USA example and that of the UK (specifically England) that accountability is being driven by a combination of performativity and market forces. It is consequential accountability. Further to these discussions on standardisation and accountability in terms of student learning outcomes there are also others that are in relation to the management of the school itself. Operational authority for schools to manage themselves is an international trend.

Devolution in the context of school-based management is a common practice in education whereby schools are allocated a global budget that they are required to employ and account for. In Victoria, an Australian state, for example, there is a 107-page document (DET Victoria 2004) that outlines in precise terms how monies are to be distributed to cover leadership and staffing needs, teaching support, maintenance of premises, calculating on-costs, students with disabilities, students with special learning needs, English as a second language, rurality and isolation and priority programmes. Schools in Victoria are held accountable for managing their budgets to cover these various exigencies. Each of which, in turn, is subject to a plethora of regulations and frameworks.

In recent years there has been a steady accretion or layering of devolved accountability to schools that are required to be concerned about matters as diverse as occupational health and safety issues and monitoring of resources and assets as well as student learning outcomes. And yet, paradoxically, while they are responsible for them they have little control over the policy regimes that govern how they are to operate.

Responsibility

What is it to be a responsible professional in an education context? In an address to the European Reading Conference Schleicher (2007) of the OECD has argued that Australia's PISA literacy results placed it in the top tier of countries along with Finland and Canada, and that this was the consequence of high levels of professional responsibility. A mark of professional responsibility is such that practitioners should not, as Freiesleben and Pohl (2004) put it, 'limit their focus only to rationally perceivable conditions' (p.1209) as would be required of them under some of the crude accountability mechanisms discussed above, but rather should strive for quality as a form of moral responsibility. They argue that applying moral principles to professional action calls for courage, honesty and strength, as indeed we have in Chapter 3. Furthermore, they make the case for professional autonomy, stating that 'there is no such thing as responsibility without independence from the say of others' (p.1215) and conclude their provocative article written mainly for a corporate audience by claiming that 'the concept of economics should be subordinated to the more fundamental concept of ethics' (p.1216).

Professional responsibility, for us, transcends accountability in its appeal to moral behaviours carried out by agents who see themselves as having the authority to address the ethical maxims laid out by Ahmed and Machold (2004) and discussed earlier in this chapter. Educational professionals exercising moral responsibility would certainly see themselves striving for quality and being publicly accountable, but to a set of standards that are morally defensible and which are exercised freely, unconstrained by either censure or praise, but guided by a belief that what is being undertaken is justifiably in the interests of those receiving the educational service.

So, how might this look in the messy world of practice and teacher inquiry in the interests of professional learning? Here we examine a case that one of us has been involved in as an academic partner, facilitating the inquiry.

Accountability Versus Professional Responsibility at Marius High School[2]

Marius High School is situated in a major Australian city on the coastal fringe. It is a comprehensive, coeducational school and relatively small. Alongside the school is a primary school, a number of whose students will go on to the High School. These two schools, along with several others and a number of environmental education facilities are members of a small network which has been assembled in order to examine ways of better understanding issues around climate change and its consequences, from the local to the global.

The collective has received some funding from the relevant state government, a condition of which was that they specifically focus upon the middle years of schooling and the transition from primary to secondary school. While this could be seen to be highly desirable, it is also problematic for several reasons, one of which is that in an educational markets environment students from the primary schools do not necessarily graduate to the local secondary schools, so that developing programmes that build on the primary school experience may only have relevance for a proportion of the younger learners. The second difficulty is that Marius High School, along with most others in that state has a strongly segmented curriculum, driven by highly specific syllabus requirements; so that establishing a programme that grows out of the work of the primary schools and continues to integrate learning around issues in relation to climate change questions is very difficult.

Of course Marius High School is not alone in working under these conditions. In their reflections on the nature of secondary schooling in England, Fielding et al. (2007) have observed that 'secondary schooling is conducted in a mindset that is

---

[2]The name of the school and the programme have been fictionalised. As a form of 'membership check' we invited several of the participants in the project to agree to its general tenor and contents, which they have done.

dangerously anachronistic and deeply superficial' (p.5). And so it is in most Australian States and territories and many parts of North America. Secondary schools are 'stuck' in early twentieth-century conditions with their isolated departmental silos operating as sovereign states.

In situations such as this the academic partner plays the role of critical friend, bringing to attention some of the very real dilemmas that are being confronted in an environment where these tensions are normally undisclosed, but exist nonetheless. The professional learning of the practitioners revolves not only around designing a pedagogical project, but also in relation to communicating effectively both within the school and within the networked learning community - a challenge hitherto not experienced.

The High School situation is illustrative of the difficulties faced by those who are necessarily accountable to the employing authority but wishing to act in a professionally responsible manner. The participants in the project hold strong feelings about climate change and the impact that the behaviour of each of us has upon it. They desire that their students will be well informed, will take an inquiry stance, and will build on prior experiences from the earlier years. But they are required to meet specific syllabus outcomes that are tightly constructed and subject to surveillance. They perceive that they need longer blocks of learning time, but this would require timetable adjustments that face them and their colleagues with great difficulties. It is imagined that the school would benefit from one or some teachers coming from a primary teaching background to assist in re-imagining the middle years, but the school is required to deal with staffing formulae that clearly establish who may and may not teach in the secondary years.

In addition to these challenges, the teachers involved in the project are aware that not all of their colleagues share their commitment to investigating climate change and its consequences and see them as having access to forms of professional development over a sustained period of time (3 years) that are not available to all. With such a large task ahead of them the secondary school team do not have a great deal of time to devote to bringing their colleagues alongside them, but perceive that it is a necessary part of the process. Of course, this case is not an isolated instance, as we outline in Chapter 7. Innnovation requires practitioners to confront the persistent structures that surround them, and this can be risky business.

Conclusion

This brief case is offered as an example of where accountability and professional responsibility intersect and go their respective ways. Clearly, in terms of being in a funded project, there are a number of accountability requirements that the teachers have to meet: they must account for the time and resources that they have devoted to the project and they must also be accountable for meeting syllabus outcomes determined by an external body. At the intersection they must be both accountable and professionally responsible in interacting with their peers such that professional learning can occur for all as well as attending to the ongoing learning needs of their students.

In being professionally responsible they must also have a belief that their work is honourable and moral, and that it meets the maxims of quality of which we have written so much in this chapter. If, as we assert, quality is to be reclaimed as a genuine virtue, then genuinely meeting accountability and professional responsibility standards is central, but in the former case it is not sufficient. In the end, quality will be determined by the extent to which professional responsibility is enacted.

Part III
Tensions, Contradictions, Competing Agendas

Chapter 7
What Is at Stake and What Is at Risk

> *One of the most frequent complaints of supervisors or principals is that too many teachers are not creative or innovative, but adhere slavishly to the curriculum despite pleas emphasizing freedom.*
>
> (Sarason 1971: 48)

> *(What is required) is that schoolteachers accept the obligation as a group to develop a forum specifically devoted to their growth and development, a forum that acknowledges that there is a world of ideas, theory, research and practice about which they should be knowledgeable (which is not to say expert) if they are not to wither on the vine, if they like their students are to avoid passive resignation to routine.*
>
> (Sarason 1996: 369)

These two quotes from the prolific writings of Seymour Sarason are a kind of dialogue between his original book *The Culture of the School and the Problem of Change* and his subsequent publication *Revisiting The Culture of the School and the Problem of Change*, which he wrote 25 years later. Drawing on his own well-known adage 'the more things change, the more they remain the same', Sarason puzzles as to why educational practices show little evidence of growing in new and different directions. In some ways, in his revisitation, he answers his own question that unless teachers collectively admit to their need for ongoing professional learning that takes them across the career span and that requires them to be actively and intellectually engaged, their practice will become moribund.

In this chapter we seek to examine what is at stake and what is at risk in terms of teacher professional learning. We also address the additional riskiness that is involved when young people themselves are consulted about their schooling experiences and the ways in which these perceptions might impact upon how teachers might act, a matter we briefly touched upon in Chapter 3.

S. Groundwater-Smith and N. Mockler, *Teacher Professional Learning in an Age of Compliance*, DOI: 10.1007/978-1-4020-9417-0_7,
© Springer Science + Business Media B.V. 2009

What Is at Stake?

So what is at stake here? If teachers are not to be trapped by the 'regularities' of schooling, that is the norms and routines that govern daily practice, they will need to be defiant, that is, they will need the courage to challenge the well-established mores of practice - the kind of courage that was discussed in Chapter 3. What constitutes teaching and schooling in the English-speaking world is well established. It is governed by a pragmatic view of the purposes of schooling being principally instrumental, that is, preparing young people to engage in the world of work, of commerce and of politics in such a way that they will fit easily into that world and undertake the roles and tasks that are assigned to them.

Of course practice is not a single act but a bundle of activities that take place in a well-established social field, in this case education. It is the practitioner's actual, daily embodied activity, including skills, tacit knowledge and presuppositions, as well as his or her social and professional interaction with others and with material and other resources. What takes place in the practitioner's head is also moderated by each individual's professional, social and political history. Practice in any profession is a many-layered and complex phenomenon, which is both purpose-oriented and norm-oriented; it encompasses mental, social and physical activities and codes:

> A 'practice' (Praktik) is a routinized type of behaviour which consists of several elements, interconnected to one another: forms of bodily activities, forms of mental activities, 'things' and their use, a background knowledge in the form of understanding, know-how, state of emotion and motivational knowledge. (Reckwitz 2002: 249)

Reckwitz distinguishes here, in the German sense between practice as *Praxis*, as human action, and as *Praktiken*, a theory of social practices. Kemmis (2008) sees the former in a more elaborated form as

> action that comes together and coheres in the context of a way of life, a way of orienting oneself in any and all of the uncertain situations we encounter. An act that is praxis is to be understood as an act in a life, an act that will or will not contribute to living one's life rightly and well. (Kemmis 2008: 2)

This view of *praxis* is guided by the key question 'how can I behave in a more educated, moral and ethical manner?'. Kemmis and Smith (2007) argue that *praxis* is shaped and formed by what they have named as *practice architectures* that are formations that determine how practice will be carried out, these being cultural and discursive preconditions, material and economic preconditions, and social and political preconditions. All these form the building blocks of practice. Schatzki (2005) calls these 'site ontologies':

> Site ontologies maintain that social life, by which I mean human coexistence, is inherently tied to a kind of context in which it transpires. The type of context involved - called 'sites' – comprises contexts of which some of what occurs or exists in them are inherently parts. The thrust of site ontology, consequently, is that human coexistence inherently transpires as part of a context of a particular sort. This thesis, in turn, implies that a certain type of context is central to analysing and explaining social phenomena. (Schatzki 2005: 467)

Schatzki goes on to explain that sites can be seen as arenas, as a part of something that exists or occurs. It is a kind of context 'that surrounds or immerses something and enjoys powers of determination with respect to it' (p.468). These sites, in both Schatzki's and Kemmis and Smith's terms, are sites of the social governed by the dispositions and habits of those who occupy them both in the present and in the past, such that the practice is perpetuated, and in some cases even solidified.

To make this a little more concrete, let us look at two examples of 'practice architectures' that might shape teacher professional learning[1]: the first a conventional 1-day course, the second a de-brief and reflection following an intervention within an action research cycle and let us ask ourselves 'what is at stake here?'

Behaviour Management – A 1-Day Course
Teachers at Burnham High School, a comprehensive, co-educational secondary school located in a large Northern city in England, had a concern for students' confronting and challenging behaviours. As a consequence a senior member of the school executive investigated the range of one-day courses that could be drawn upon to assist staff in the ways in which they might address the difficulties that they were encountering. For example, inappropriate behaviours appeared to escalate rapidly in classrooms leading to disruption and confrontation. A rapid scan of the internet of 'courses in behaviour management for teachers' revealed nearly three hundred thousand sites within 0.26 seconds. Many had the imprimatur of agencies such as the British General Teaching Council and included private corporations such as Pivotal Education who offered, among other things, tips for managing wayward behaviours http://www.pivotaleducation.com/behaviour/tips.php. Some included strategies for covert observation of young people and forms of training.

Having selected a given course in 'Turning behaviour around' a day was set aside. A consultant was employed to teach the teachers the range of interpersonal skills that should be used in classrooms to counteract the 'anti-learning' ethos of the students. A dense power-point presentation covered: changing attitudes; changing behaviour; dealing with negativity; getting students on side; and, enabling students to build self-esteem. Teachers were divided into cross-discipline groups to discuss some agreed strategies that would 'ensure consistency across the school'. Each group was required to present their strategies and a small committee was formed to collate these into an overall policy. The remainder of the day was spent focussing upon the kinds of teaching styles that teachers saw themselves employing and which contributed to a sense of professional wellbeing.

Reflecting upon Learning - Action Research and Early Career Teaching
Marianne Girls High School is located in an inner city suburb of metropolitan Sydney with a high proportion of Muslim families, a number of whom are recently arrived refugees. In common with many schools facing difficult social and economic circumstances the school has a disproportionate number of early career teachers who have only recently graduated. As a part of the school's induction policy such teachers are mentored by senior, experienced teachers and spend time in an action learning set where they investigate their classroom practices and reflect upon what might be learned.

---

[1] These cases are fictional, but constructed from our experience of working with schools in both the UK and Australia.

On the occasion reported here the group was poring over a series of photographs that had been taken during the course of a lesson. The mentor teacher took a digital photograph of where the early career teacher was in the classroom every minute of a 50 minute block of learning time. All members of the group were reflecting upon what they could see and what they thought it might mean. During the discussion a number of questions were raised: 'when you moved between the groups were you seeking out students who were clearly not on-task?' 'some students took the initiative and came to you, is it generally the same ones?' 'you never seemed to be talking to the teaching assistant who was in the classroom with you, is that because you talk afterwards, or were you avoiding her?'

In the first case, the 'practice architecture' is a familiar one. The purpose is clear: the students are to be 'managed' more effectively. The norms are consistent: 'students learn and teachers teach'. The solutions are evident, what is required is consistency. The designated roles have been assigned, the consultant instructs and the teachers respond. A policy is created, the problem is solved. All of the elements are interconnected in a predictable structured manner. It would be a courageous teacher indeed who would behave in a transgressive manner in such a context. Being subversive brings with it a range of social sanctions. While individuals may internally contest what is being said and done they will be unlikely to do other than conform to the role assigned to them, to listen to the expert, to discuss with their peers and to develop coherent and consistent strategies. Previously established patterns and routines tell them that this is how professional development is done. It is done to them by others. The process is essentially a reproductive one.

By way of contrast our second episode points to a different kind of architecture - one that is investigative. The group members are seeking to identify patterns of interaction and hypothesise what they might mean. They are unlikely to find answers, but may be able to identify a specific question that could be focused upon. The practice of the early career teacher in the frame may be remade as a result of the exposure. Thus, the process has the potential to be transformative. It could well be argued in Sarason's terms that these teachers are active and intellectually engaged.

What is at stake then is teacher professionalism - teaching as a vocation. Originally, the term 'vocation' carried with it connotations of commitment and service. Derived from the latin root, *vocare*, 'to call', it suggested selflessness and devotion to a particular form of work. For many today the word 'vocation' has a narrower utilitarian ring to it, tied as it has become to vocational training. Indeed, in the English context with its highly specified curriculum, targets and inspectorial system this may well be the case. And yet, there are still many who would contend that teaching is more than a skilled occupation, one which is unavoidably moral, and is of inestimable social worth. Hansen (1994) claims:

> To regard teaching as vocational further presumes a sense of it (however inchoate) as an activity whose meaning is larger than the sum of its parts. It is larger than carrying out a finite number of pre-specified duties and responsibilities, with a preordained set of rewards as compensation. A person enacting a vocation has an active and creative relationship with the work. The work involves initiative, rather than carrying out passively a package of discrete tasks. ... This means supplementing and possibly extending the functional requirements of the job. It may mean questioning some of those requirements. This posture implies that the person with a sense of vocation will be his or her own final critic, a stance that may accompany any work perceived as more than routine. (pp.4–5)

Partly, what is at stake, then, is the professional identity of the practitioner. How is she seen, how does she see herself? Teacher professional identity is inextricably linked to teachers' understandings of themselves as human beings, contextualised within their professional lives, insofar as a capacity to understand oneself professionally is linked to having a knowledge about oneself generally. The articulation of professional identity requires teachers to construct themselves in their own minds to start with, as teachers, but then to 'claim' a professional identity. The process of supporting teachers to articulate or think about their professional identity is one of helping them to draw the links between their own sense of vocation and their professional practice, thereby assisting them to enact their own personal 'theory' in their practice within and beyond the classroom.

What Is at Risk?

If teacher professional identity and the capacity for resistance are at stake, it follows that what is offered up as powerful professional learning is at risk. Engaging in learning that will result in challenging the wishes of those who employ teachers may be seen as very risky business indeed, especially in the current climate where there is an increasing gulf between the ways in which the factory model of schooling is conducted and the needs and wants of learners in the new millennium. We would argue that it is authentic student learning that is most at risk, the very thing that schools are allegedly designed for.

It is increasingly understood that young people, in order to productively participate in social and academic life both in and out of school, need to be active agents in that life. Unlike the adults who surround them, today's young people have been born into a digital world, they know it, they understand it and they can navigate within it - for them it is not in any way exotic, it is normal. Old models of teaching and telling are no longer sufficient for young people in our schools today, or indeed in other places where they may learn. As we noted in Chapter 4, Cornu (2004) has observed in relation to schools that knowledge is now networked and requires an understanding of a collective intelligence over and above individual enterprise. Two key concepts that are of a sociocultural nature and central to understanding how young people learn in a digital environment are *cognitive activity*, where the learner is actively engaged in both the medium and the message of learning, and *social interaction* that allows for the development, questioning and analysis of what is being learned through social and machine-mediated processes. New bridges have to be made that allow much greater learner agency.

The discussions regarding the uses of the new technologies in education have moved considerably in the last 2 decades. Much of the early work was in relation to how they might be employed for learning in terms of hardware provision; more recently, the question being asked is 'why' they should be employed. It is less a matter of what the technologies can or cannot do, but rather what are they for. As Apple (2003) has pointed out, early concerns seemed to be dominated by a pragmatic quest to enable young people to be ready for a technologically saturated workforce. Today the questions are much more sophisticated and pedagogically oriented, especially with an epistemological focus upon what kinds of knowledge are being developed by whom and for what purpose.

Learner agency was a key feature of Facer, Furlong, Furlong and Sutherland's study (2003) where they found that the majority of young people whom they interviewed and observed were very positive about their use of computers in the home, but were negative about their experiences at school, where they found that, in general, their teachers were over-prescriptive and there were limited opportunities to engage in playful discovery. The provision of information and communication technologies cannot, of themselves, stand alone. They need to be supported by sound practices that encourage learners' engagement and agency and develop in them a capacity for critical analysis and evaluation.

As a context for professional practice in education this is a very new and unfamiliar architecture; the physical school with its enclosing walls, classrooms, staffrooms, corridors and offices is no parallel for the virtual learning space of web 2.0 technologies. These sites are ones in which dexterous youngsters can undertake a huge array of activities simultaneously, and often of their own choosing. As Zevernbergen and Zevernbergen (2007) have argued:

> It is hardly surprising that Millenials (current generation) are likely to be bored with the traditional forms of school education - teacher-directed lessons; linear step-by-step logic; and the pencil-and-paper testing formats of much assessment. (p.33)

Just as it is risky for teachers to challenge the traditions of schooling and the ways in which they are best professionally prepared, so too is it risky for large school systems when young people can and do turn to other forms of authority. Partly, the risk is perceived to be one of child protection, so that unlimited access to the more shady parts of the World Wide Web is seen as problematic; but this is not the way in which it is seen by the learners themselves who believe that they are well able to manage the mesh of practices and information contained therein. The difficulty is that they are not often asked what their attitudes to such matters are.

One of the great puzzles of schooling is why the young people themselves are rarely consulted regarding the practice architectures of which they are such a critical part. In the remainder of this chapter we shall look at the case for consulting young people and the contribution that such consultation might make to teacher professional learning such that schooling might grow in new and different directions.

Why Consult Young People?

Turning to young people themselves, when we consult them and treat them seriously, whether in regard to designing the learning spaces, the organisation of the learning or the learning experiences, it is possible to develop a product or process that will have greater relevance for them and one with which they will wish to engage (Grosvenor and Burke 2008). Designing for learning must not only relate to re-conceptualising places and spaces in terms of new facilities, but equally importantly, re-examining old and sometimes 'tired' learning environments that are virtually antithetical to transformative learning. Designing for positive learning outcomes is currently being led by those who are challenging the conventions that are institution-centric and turning to those that are learner focused. What is sought is a consultative model that is flexible and responsive and accounts for the various technological convergences, new knowledge and better understanding of an interactive pedagogy (Valenti 2002).

In the school context, Burke and Grosvenor (2003) have noted: 'There is a history of not attending to the expressed experience of children within schools. Everyday neglect in this sense has become institutional.' While, in the main, it is true that schools rarely consult their students and take them seriously, there are schools both in the UK and in Australia where there have been systematic policies and practices that have enabled students' voices to be heard and have even given students agency in designing, investigating, analysing and interpreting learning and conditions for learning (Groundwater-Smith and Mockler 2003b).

Mitra (2004) has argued that where students have agency, a sense of belonging, and are recognised as competent, they gain a stronger sense of their own abilities and build awareness that they can make changes in their schools, not only for themselves, but also for others. In the past, however, the young people themselves were either not consulted at all, or were, at best, treated only as a data source. Raymond (2001) has noted that there are three further steps that can be taken: *discussion*, where young people are active respondents; *dialogue*, where they are co-researchers; and, *significant voice*, where they are researchers, initiating, inquiring, interpreting and developing actions.

In his analysis of the very real difficulties in consulting young people, Fielding (2004b) reminds us of the range of practical concerns that we must address if we are to move forward in giving them that significant voice to which Raymond (2001) alluded.

> (We need to) resist the constant pull for either 'fadism' or 'manipulative incorporation'. ... Fadism leads to unrealistic expectations, subsequent marginalisation and the unwitting corrosion of integrity; manipulative incorporation leads to betrayal of hope, resigned exhaustion and the bolstering of an increasingly powerful status quo. (Fielding 2004: 296)

He asks a series of penetrating questions, among them the following:

- How confident are we that our research does not redescribe and reconfigure students in ways that bind them more securely into the fabric of the status quo?
- How clear are we about the use to which the depth and detail of data is likely to be put? Is our more detailed knowledge of what students think and feel largely used to help us control them more effectively?
- Are we sure that our positions of relative power and our own personal and professional interests are not blurring our judgements or shaping our advocacy? (pp.302–304)

In our publication *Learning to Listen: Listening to Learn* (Groundwater-Smith and Mockler 2003), we refer to the Coalition of Knowledge Building Schools (CKBS) a consortium of schools that have a commitment to listening and acting upon the voices of young people. In more recent years, the Coalition has grown to include

13 schools: primary and secondary; government and independent; as well as cultural sites that offer education beyond the classroom. A repertoire of practices has been developed. Principal of these is focus group discussion, conducted by both adults and students who have been previously trained.

As Colucci (2007) has observed focus group discussions can be fun, enjoyable, successful and rich in in-depth data. Because they are interactive in nature they have a capacity to open up issues in ways that individual interviews cannot. Four distinctive methods have been employed by Coalition schools and institutions: visual metaphors, musical metaphors, photography and drawing. In the first case, a series of visual images might be presented to a group of young people with a specific tag such as 'which of these images relate to the ways in which you learn in small groups in school?' After recording their individual thoughts, students have a wide-ranging discussion of how they responded and why. Similarly, using music, a number of very short pieces are played and students are asked to select one that accords with their feelings or attitudes to a particular phenomenon such as the use of poetry in the English classroom. In the latter two instances, using photography and drawing, students undertake an activity prior to the focus group discussion, such as photographing places that are helpful/unhelpful to their learning or drawing themselves using computers at school and at home.

Colucci cites a number of other activities that serve to stimulate discussion such as:

- Developing lists (why one should or should not engage in a particular activity)
- Rating items, words, objects and pictures
- Ranking terms from 'most' to 'least'
- Sorting piles
- Choosing among alternatives
- Labelling key words, objects and pictures
- Using fantasy
- Storytelling
- Creating a news bulletin
- Role playing

When encouraged to be fully participative and included in the subsequent analysis, students are most giving. Importantly, they wish to see that the inquiry has an effect. If, for example, they disclose that their secondary school classes are ones where bullying among students and between students and teachers is the norm and following the inquiry nothing changes, then they rapidly become cynical and disillusioned. At the same time, it is unlikely that the changes that may result from the inquiry would greatly impact upon the overall practice architecture within the school in that the hierarchical management of the school, its organisation into faculties and its arrangements for assessment would probably remain untouched.

Some schools in the Coalition have gone as far as to consult the young people about their teachers' professional learning, asking them what they understand such learning to be and how teachers go about improving their classroom practices. Many students in the secondary sector have been puzzled by the concept that their teachers may go on learning about their practice; they believe that if learning is happening surely practice should be changing as a result. When probed about teachers going away from the classroom for courses, the view seems to be that they were only aware of such attendance because for that period a casual or supply teacher was provided. Seemingly, the practice architecture is such that short interventions make little difference. By way of contrast, primary school students were more alert to their teachers being learners; some suggested that they learned as a result of observing and listening in terms of what happened in classrooms and acting upon that knowledge. It may well be that the context of the primary school is such that the relationship is a more sustained one and that just as teachers may observe their students, so too can the students observe their teachers.

Our discussion thus far focuses, in the main, on students as consultants, with the inference that asking for students' perspectives is necessarily a liberatory practice. However, as Rudduck and McIntyre (2007) have cautioned us, not all consultation is designed to such ends. In England, a number of schools are now convening student advisory groups to inform inspectorial visits and are more to do with teacher/school performativity than provide insights into practice such that it might be improved. The hijacking of 'student voice' to these ends is a very real prospect. Indeed, the statutory guidance (DfES 2004) requires head teachers, governors and local education authorities to 'give young children and young people a say'. As Arnot and Reay have observed, student voices that are heard in the process of consultation 'are not in fact independently constructed "voices"', rather they are 'the messages created by *particular pedagogic contexts*[2] (p.317).

However, as we have hinted, students can be more than consultants; they can be researchers who use the tools of inquiry, analyse the data, construct arguments and defend their subsequent knowledge claims. Thomson and Gunter (2007) present a fine case study of students investigating bullying through photo-elicitation and verbal scenarios. What emerged were multiple perspectives of activity in the classroom and wider school.

> School students 'know', and they do have specific perspective(s) which is/are not the same as that of teachers. But, students' and teachers' knowledges are diverse, and in some cases overlap between the two perspectives. The issue for us as academic researchers working with students remains the creation of research practices which honour but do not romanticise or unnecessarily privilege the points of view of students, while at the same time shifting the generational power relations in the school. (p.339)

When students become researchers, there is a greater likelihood that they will also have greater agency. When, for example, students analyse questionnaires and digitally generate graphics that can be used for discussion, there is a transparency hitherto unimagined. There is an implicit permission for students to engage in discussing matters of practice - how did they originate, how are they perpetuated? Even so, we must concede that it is difficult for them to imagine something different from that in which they are already incorporated.

---

[2] Authors' emphasis

As noted above, Arnot and Reay (2007) argue that young people as students in schools speak a language that has been created for them by school pedagogies, or what we term the practice architectures of schooling. They quote Bernstein (2000) in his use of the phrase '*the acoustic of the school*' (xxi in Bernstein, p.321 in Arnot and Reay) to remind us that the codes of schooling are powerful and embedded. Alterations in one feature of practice take place within a context of continuity. In effect, stasis is the norm.

Conclusion

Teacher professional learning is but a part of the practice architecture of schooling. The complex interlocking of those cultural and discursive preconditions, material and economic preconditions, and social and political preconditions of which Kemmis and Smith (2007) write all contribute to its composition. Schatzki (2005: 480) reminds us that practices are 'nonindividualistic phenomena', but they do 'inject a deep dimension of commonality in social life'. In this chapter we have argued that in essence, when considering the ways in which teachers may engage in professional learning, what is at stake is the professional identity of the teachers as they struggle to accommodate to, or resist, the persistent structures that surround them. What is at risk is the kind of professional learning that may threaten and question those structures; this is even more so when the radical step of genuinely seeking student participation through research is undertaken.

As we have argued in previous chapters, teachers need to have courage and preparedness for defiance. It is essential that they have an understanding of what is at stake and what is at risk. It is rare in the formal provisions that are made for teacher professional learning, for example, through courses or funded projects, for these matters to be made explicit, let alone debated and contested. Individual teachers, usually unknowingly, are implicated in the development of practices that fit into the current political rationality. They are constructed as component parts of a larger machine and their contribution determined and measured through procedures that control their capacity for resistance and activism. A significant message of this book is a crie-de-cœur for the exercise, on the part of teachers, of increased imagination and inventiveness when exploring what is in the best interests of their professional practice. As Halpin (2003) has observed, there is a need for a utopian imagination if hope for the future is to be generated and nourished.

Chapter 8
Who Pays the Piper? Agendas, Priorities and Accountabilities

> *But does the school effectiveness movement, along with all its policy trappings, have anything to do with the real world? I have argued elsewhere...that we are living in a simulacrum of education constructed by the rhetoric of policy makers and reinforced by our own collusion as researchers and practitioners. I would like to argue further...that we are in danger of living in, and co-creating, a simulacrum of research whose primary purpose is not to question or to critique but to serve policy: A dangerous position that brings with it not only "the strange death of educational autonomy" (Beck 1999: 223) but also vital ethical questions to be answered about the nature, purpose and conduct of research itself.*
>
> (Atkinson 2004: 114)

In Chapter 2 we raised the proliferation over the past decade of the employment of teacher research or practitioner inquiry as a tool of policy implementation, in the UK and Australia in particular, as an issue of concern. In this chapter we build upon these observations and consider the impact of agendas, priorities and accountabilities upon the ways in which teacher professional learning is constructed, and particularly the implementation and outcomes of inquiry-based approaches to teacher professional learning within schools.

Atkinson, in the quotation reproduced above, as well as elsewhere in her recent writing, argues vehemently against the compliance agenda within education, which she sees manifest in examples where particular policy agendas (such as those of efficiency and effectiveness in particular) guide educational practice, rather than sound educational practice and knowledge about education established through research informing and forming educational policy. While for Atkinson the simulacrum of educational practice remains separate from that of research (despite their obvious links), for us the simulacra converge in the context of practitioner research. Furthermore, considering the "epidemic of quality" (Clarke and Newman 1997) which has characterised the past decade and its impact upon education as discussed at length in Chapter 6, the issue of the nature, purpose and conduct of (practitioner) research has a "quality" dimension to it as well. As we have argued elsewhere (Groundwater-Smith

S. Groundwater-Smith and N. Mockler, *Teacher Professional Learning in an Age of Compliance*, DOI: 10.1007/978-1-4020-9417-0_8,
© Springer Science+Business Media B.V. 2009

and Mockler 2006, 2008), however, and will continue to do here, measures of "quality" in the context of practitioner inquiry are distinct from those which relate to research emanating from the academy.

In this chapter we focus upon issues of purpose, evidence, effect and ethics in relation to inquiry-based professional learning. We aim to extend issues raised in Chapter 2 relating to the "legitimacy" and validity of practitioner inquiry and those raised in Chapter 6 relating to "quality" dimensions of teacher research to examine the confluence of these four areas and their implications for professional learning and education more broadly. Some years ago, one of us, writing with Judyth Sachs, posed a range of critical questions regarding the purpose, processes and outcomes of action research, which speak to the required conditions for good, valid and authentic practitioner inquiry. It was argued that questions of purpose and intent, evidence and process and action and effect could provide a lever for the kinds of accountability and validity structures which would support such practitioner inquiry. The questions posed then were as listed below.

Questions of purpose and intent:

- Who sets the research agenda and questions?
- Does the research endeavour seek to problem solve or problematise or both?
- Whose interests are served?
- How does the evidence contribute to a broad political initiative/interaction?

Questions of evidence and process:

- What kind of evidence is collected?
- Once collected, how is the evidence approached?
- How representative is the evidence of the field or population?
- How is the evidence collected?
- How transparent are the processes?

Questions of action and effect:

- How far do those involved hold the requisite power to disseminate and act upon findings?
- What are the consequences, are they manufactured or real? (Mockler and Sachs 2002: 3)

These questions give a clue as to how to conduct teacher inquiry which serves the priorities and agendas of teachers and schools, although we wish to argue here that these are by no necessity mutually exclusive from those of policy makers and funding bodies. Furthermore, building on our recent work on the confluence of quality and ethics in practitioner enquiry (Groundwater-Smith and Mockler 2006, 2008), we here wish to add a further set of guiding questions, namely those related to ethics and quality.

Questions of ethics and quality:

- How far does it explicitly observe ethical protocols and processes?
- How far is the research collaborative in its nature?

- How far can the research justify itself to its community of practice?
- How far is the research transformative in its aims?

This chapter is divided into four sections, each focusing on one of these four sets of questions. It links to the case studies in the chapters which follow, and suggests that while compromise and negotiation might often characterise the establishment and implementation of inquiry-based professional learning initiatives, these conditions do not necessarily mean that quality, ethics or outcomes are compromised in the process.

Purpose and Intent

To meet the definition of the term "professional learning", inquiry-based professional learning - indeed we would hazard *all* teacher professional learning - needs to be about improving student learning outcomes. Of course, as an intent this falls into the category of "easy to say, hard to do", and a great deal of research energy has been expended in recent years divining the links between teacher professional learning and improved student learning. Regardless of the difficulty in ascertaining links between the two on a large-scale level, there remains the necessity of formulating and forming on a small and local-scale practitioner inquiry, which aims to contribute to the improvement of student learning *in this context at this time.*

While the notion of "inquiry as stance" raised in Chapter 5 suggests the importance and indeed power of integrating inquiry processes into all aspects of "the way we do things around here" in schools, for many schools the process of engaging in inquiry-based professional learning begins on a small scale, with project funding gained from an outside body such as a government department, local education authority or professional association. On a whole-school level, the capacity for such work to be "scaled up" into broader inquiry initiatives is often contingent upon the success of the project as perceived by teachers and the school community - how far it is seen to be a significant professional learning experience, worth the expenditure of time and energy on the part of team members and substantial in terms of its impact upon student learning, for example. These indictors of success, in turn, are linked largely to the purpose and intent of the project - how far its intent was linked to the particular needs of the students, teachers and the school context and the extent to which it "made a difference".

This idea that the intent of such projects should be differentiated so as to be tailored to context and local needs generally sits uncomfortably with doctrines of compliance. Essentially, we see the compliance agenda manifest in aiming to dictate the focus of project work and replicate "what works" across a multitude of diverse and in some instances vastly different sites. In this case the capacity for teachers to take agency in their learning and in fashioning their inquiry into an investigation of issues at play within their classrooms and schools, which are of critical concern to them, can be significantly curtailed.

It is of critical importance that both the focus of the inquiry and also the questions, which guide the inquiry are established at a local level out of local issues and concerns, but this does not mean that externally established focus areas for practitioner inquiry cannot also be met. Indeed, while it may require some skill on the part of team members, capacity to "serve both masters" (i.e. the school community and the external funding body) is great in the case of most externally funded inquiry-based professional learning.

In their recent work, Caro-Bruce, Flessner, Klehr and Zeichner (2007) provide many examples of how an action research initiative developed by a large school district, in this case the Madison Metropolitan School District in Wisconsin, and designed to focus upon pedagogy was implemented in a broad variety of ways with a huge diversity of research focus questions. Some of the areas under investigation in schools and reported upon by teachers in *Creating Equitable Classrooms Through Action Research* (Caro-Bruce et al. 2007) include motivation for high school dropouts and associated student engagement issues (Shager 2007), pedagogical strategies for improving English language learners' capacity to comprehend oral directions (Richards 2007), the impact of service learning on students' self-concept and academic achievement (Kavaloski 2007) and strategies for enhancing student collaboration beyond friendship groups in the classroom (Coccari 2007). While the projects all respond to concerns and issues identified by classroom teachers and seek to gather data and "make sense" of the issue in context, they are vastly different in their focus and in the way that focus was developed. What they share is a commitment to the inquiry process and a broad focus on education for social justice and equity. As the editors note in the introductory chapter:

> While covering a variety of pedagogical topics, the studies share a common focus on equity, race and closing gaps in academic achievement between groups of students. These stories, which range in scope from a close study of one child and how his elementary teacher adapted instructional practices to ensure school success to a study of how a high school science department changed inclusive practices in an effort to eliminate tracking, illustrate the kinds of changes teachers can make in their own thinking and pedagogy on behalf of their students. (Caro-Bruce and Klehr 2007: 3)

In a similar but different manner, the 100 schools involved in the Australian Commonwealth Government-funded Innovation and Best Practice Project (IBPP) were required to undertake practitioner inquiry relating to a school-identified "innovation" in the areas of Early Literacy, Mathematics, Information and Communication Technologies and the Middle Years of Schooling. While the intent of school-based projects fed into the broader intent around studying successful innovation within school contexts, within this schools determined their own focus designed to serve local needs (DEST 2001). For many schools, including a number of those who later became members of the Coalition of Knowledge Building Schools (see Chapter 11), this meant that the project provided not only a wealth of evidence upon which decision making in the classroom and elsewhere could be based, but also a catalyst for further and more sustained inquiry-based professional learning within the school. Both the purposes of the IBPP and the schools' internal purposes were thus served.

On the other hand, Hardy and Lingard (2008) issue a guide to "traps for young players" with regard to government-funded inquiry-based professional learning initiatives in the form of their observation that policy imperatives can sometimes reach beyond the framework of the project to impinge upon the ways in which teachers can and do engage in professional learning.

Evidence and Process

Elsewhere we have written at length regarding evidence in practitioner inquiry - adversarial, forensic and historical approaches. We have chosen to reproduce some of this earlier thinking here by way of illustrating the development of the ideas contained in this work over the past years:

> We believe that we can think of the purposes for gathering evidence in three ways. The first of these is to use the evidence in adversarial settings where it is utilised to prove a case. Those seeking for that elusive, indeed we would argue impossible, goal "best practice" would wish to prove that one method is indisputably better than another. Thus, in medicine, using randomised control trials, there are those that seek for the "best treatment" irrespective of the multitude of variables within any medical condition. Similarly education has been beset by the "best practice" holy grail; as if it is possible to identify one best way, for example, to teach reading, or counter bullying in schools, or induct new and beginning teachers in isolated schools.

> The second purpose for gathering evidence is to conceive of it within a discourse of forensic science, where the investigator is seeking above all else to understand a particular phenomenon. Knowledge building organisations clearly wish to achieve a deep understanding of that which happens within them: teaching and learning; managing human and material resources; communication and participation; and so on. Of course, this does not mean that practitioner enquiry should not concern itself with the quality of evidence, but rather the purposes to which that evidence is to be put. Norris & Robinson (2001) quite properly point out that a distinction should be made between weak and strong evidence.

> There is a third conceptualisation of evidence which has been largely unexplored in the context of practitioner enquiry. This is the notion of re-examining and re-interpreting evidence as an historian would. Evidence from past events can be re-thought and re-told in the light of new knowledge. For example, Davis (2001) developed an argument that late nineteenth century policies with respect to famines in the Indian subcontinent, Africa and China, were based upon precepts which argued that the indigenous people were indolent and unsatisfactory land managers and did not deserve support because they brought about the famines themselves. By re-examining the data on climate through an understanding of El Nino he has argued that the policies were morally unsustainable. Knowledge building organisations need to not only think about present events, but also to reflect on the organisation's past history and how this affects and influences what is happening today. (Groundwater-Smith and Mockler 2002: 2)

Clearly, we position ourselves as advocates of a forensic or historical approach to the collection and use of evidence: indeed this is the approach we have worked with educators to promote in a vast range of different school contexts. It is our belief that these approaches provide the greatest scope in terms of opening up spaces for discussion and debate, providing teachers with scope for a range of interpretations, and foster high levels of collaboration.

Questions of evidence and process relate not only to the conceptualisation of evidence which frames the practitioner research initiative, but also to the places in which, and the methods by which, evidence is collected in practitioner inquiry. While the research endeavour is not, we believe, intrinsically difficult, it is important that teachers undertaking inquiry are equipped with the skills and knowledge they need to make judgements about where and how to look for evidence, and it is here that a critical friend or academic partner can lend support and work to build capacity within the School. A range of projects funded by NSW state and Australian Federal Government initiatives over the past decade (including the IBPP example cited above) have made use of this model whereby an individual with well-developed skills in research as well as expertise in the focus area for research provides professional development support for school-based teams. The academic partner or critical friend provides particular support in terms of the *processes* of inquiry, where often team members have limited experience and capability at the outset. The notion of the critical friend and their role within inquiry-based professional learning will be taken up further in Chapter 9.

Action and Effect

Teacher inquiry is in its very nature transformative in its intent. In particular, it aims to transform teaching and learning, but those of us who have worked for many years with and around teachers who are active and passionate inquirers know of the capacity it has to transform teachers and also students themselves, as well as provide learning opportunities for the academic partner (Groundwater-Smith and Mockler 2009, forthcoming).

Questions of action and effect relate to how far practitioner inquiry holds the capacity to transform the school environment - how far the players hold the power and authority to make decisions and act upon the findings, and how robust and authentic the findings are in the first place. Where the findings of practitioner inquiry initiatives relate solely to the classrooms of participants, the level of agency in terms of acting upon findings is likely to be far greater than in those instances where the findings have implications for schools or systems more broadly.

Whatever the context, the resolution of these questions of action and effect depends upon the commitment of practitioner researchers to take action, regardless of how confronting or uncomfortable the findings may be. Some years ago Marion Dadds observed the difficulty and complexity that practitioner inquiry can sometimes bring:

> [In self-study] we may be entering into processes by which we deconstruct some basic, historically rooted views of ourselves. In such processes our existing images of the professional self will be challenged, questioned, re-thought and re-shaped in some degree. These processes are necessary if change and development are to occur and self-study is to lead to new learning. We cannot escape them, nor the discomfort they may bring if we value our commitment to professional development. (Dadds 1993: 288)

Furthermore, the successful resolution of these questions of action and effect also rely upon school leaders and their willingness to take seriously the outcomes of inquiry and support teachers to take action, even in cases where doing so might cut against the grain of compliance and require the sponsoring of calculated risks.

Quality and Ethics

Almost a decade ago Peter Foster (1999) criticised teacher research funded by the United Kingdom's (as it was then known) Teacher Training Agency for taking a "never mind the quality, feel the impact" approach to research and inquiry. Foster's criticism was a response to the "what works" agenda and the drive at the time to make educational research all about relevance and practical application; however, one cannot help but feel that in conceptualising research as somehow being handed from the academy to practitioners as part of the instrumentalist agenda Foster has somehow missed the point of practitioner inquiry as professional development. He does, however, raise some interesting issues around quality and validity in teacher research, which link to our claim, expressed in Chapter 2 at some length, that practitioner inquiry sits alongside that which emanates from the academy as a different, not lesser, sibling.

Our argument about ethics as a quality test for practitioner inquiry has been made at length elsewhere (Groundwater-Smith and Mockler 2006, 2008). In a nutshell, we believe that practitioner research should be led by a series of broad overarching ethical guidelines, which in their enactment support "quality" in such research:

- *That it should observe ethical protocols and processes*: Practitioner research is subject to the same ethical protocols as other social research. Informed consent should be sought from participants, whether students, teachers, parents or others, and an earnest attempt should be made to "do no harm".
- *That it should be transparent in its processes*: One of the broader aims of practitioner research lies in the building of community and the sharing of knowledge and ideas. To this end, practitioner research should be "transparent" in its enactment, and practitioner researchers accountable to their community for the processes and products of their research. Publication (whether to the "village" or to the "world" [Stenhouse 1981: 17]) is part of this transparency, as is the opening of the research to vigorous dialogue and debate.
- *That it should be collaborative in its nature*: Practitioner research should aim to provide opportunities for colleagues to share, discuss and debate aspects of their practice in the name of improvement and development. The responsible "making sense" of data collected from within the field of one's own practice (through triangulation of evidence and other means) relies heavily on these opportunities.
- *That it should be able to justify itself to its community of practice*: Engaging in practitioner research involves an opportunity cost to the community. To do well requires time and energy that cannot be spent in other professional ways. The benefits must be commensurable with the effort and resources expended in the course of the work, which necessarily will require collaboration and communication.
- *That it should be transformative in its intent and action*: Practitioner researchers engage in an enterprise, which is, in essence, about contributing to both transformation of practice and transformation of society. As Marion Dadds (1998) writes:

> At the heart of every practitioner research project there is a significant job of work to be done that will make a small contribution to the improvement of the human condivtion in that

context. Good practitioner research, I believe, helps to develop life for others in caring, equitable, humanising ways. (Groundwater-Smith and Mockler 2008)

For us, responsible and ethical practitioner research operates in such a way as to create actionable, actioned outcomes, and the critical questions relating to quality and ethics thus link at each stage of the inquiry process to those of purpose and intent, evidence and process and action and effect.

Conclusion

What do we "buy into" in inquiry-based professional learning? For all stakeholders there is a cost, whether it is the opportunity cost in terms of time and energy expended by teachers and students, or the financial cost contributed by governments and bureaucracies who have appropriated the notion of practitioner inquiry and sponsor it in schools to their own ends. So what exactly is it that stakeholders think they are purchasing?

For governments and bureaucracies the purchase is largely about being seen to contribute to the learning of the teaching profession, and specifically to the growth of "evidence-based practice", a catch-cry of compliance. Further, it can be seen as a tool of policy implementation, where schools are provided with resourcing for the purpose of using the inquiry process to implement policy directions in schools and classrooms. For teachers and schools, however (who arguably have greater purchasing power), the transaction is a very different one, and one which they largely enter into because of the capacity for this work to contribute to their learning and their professional knowledge and to create improvements in learning for their students. In order for this to happen in such a way that the transaction represents "value" for these stakeholders, it is essential, as we have argued, for the work to be differentiated and tailored to local concerns and needs. We have tried to show in this chapter, however, that these two sets of requirements, while we place the greatest importance on those of teachers and schools, need not be mutually exclusive.

Chapter 9
What Learning Community?
A Knotty Problem

> *Sites of inter-organisational collaboration are characterised as 'knots': a loose network of actors, practices and systems that does not have a centre, and in which the only consistency over time is the ongoing mix of interaction among contributors, discourses, tasks and tools.... New learning challenges are presented as actors struggle to make a sense of unfamiliar situations in the knots, improvise collaborative practices and negotiate the politics of colliding knowledge systems and interests of multiple organizations. In particular, different organisational discourses and discursive strategies encounter one another, and must be negotiated somehow by the organisational actors working in the knots.*

(Fenwick 2007: 139)

There can be no question that Etienne Wenger's seminal work *Communities of Practice: Learning, Meaning and Identity* (1998) has had a significant impact upon workplace learning and knowledge construction that goes beyond the individual. The publication has captured the notion that the kind of dynamic co-constructed knowledge held in and across organizations can make a difference to those working in them and that this knowledge can produce a shared repertoire of practices such as routines, responses, tools and the like. For a number of years now, in education, learning communities have had a place, although they may not have been named as Communities of Practice and much has been made of both the learning communities themselves and the ways in which they can relate, one with another, in networks and partnerships. In this chapter we shall explore the basic tenets of Communities of Practice, Professional Learning Communities and Networked Learning Communities in the context of providing for teacher professional learning based upon inquiry. We shall examine the conditions that facilitate and impede such communities and will argue that their configurations are knotlike, complex and difficult to unravel.

S. Groundwater-Smith and N. Mockler, *Teacher Professional Learning in an Age of Compliance*, DOI: 10.1007/978-1-4020-9417-0_9,
© Springer Science+Business Media B.V. 2009

Communities of Practice and How They Operate

Imagine for a moment a group of teachers working in different schools under
different regimes. They have a common interest in issues around climate change
and sustainability and meet informally to discuss ways in which they may ensure
that their students are alerted to the current concerns and challenges ranging from
the local to the global. They all have read deeply in the field. Some are secondary
teachers with interests in science and technology; some are from primary schools,
accustomed to teaching across a range of curriculum areas in a holistic and
integrated fashion. They all wish to create, refine and communicate what they know
and understand in relation to climate change and sustainability. They have agreed
to investigate with their students what *they* currently know and understand and to
see whether they might apply for some funding to develop a project based upon
what they have so far discovered.

Think of a group of senior education bureaucrats. They work in different parts of
a large state-based system. They meet irregularly to consider how their various
departments are coping with the ever-changing digital environment. They are concerned
with how different regulatory frameworks, constructed within departments, can
collide with each other when seen overall. In one department there is a perceived
need to control student access to digital resources in the interests of child protection,
whereas in another, there are concerns about ways in which student access could be
increased in the interests of equity. While they do not have a formal brief that
requires them to meet together they can see that by increasing the flow of information from one department to another, more coherent policies might be formulated.

In both of these cases, it can be argued that Communities of Practice are being
formed. They are basically self-organising, social, and relate to professional learning
issues that matter to the participants. They share a common vocabulary and engage
in joint activities, albeit as a result of their own initiatives. They are flexible and
adaptable because they are not seeking to satisfy an externally mandated purpose.
We can also say what they are not – they are not a team that is task-based; they are
not an organised professional learning community; they are not a network (although
they could become one); and they are neither officially sanctioned nor under scrutiny.
They are not there to be micro-managed. Their professional knowledge is owned
by them and they work at the boundaries rather than at the core of the operation.

While self-sufficiency is an earmark of a successful Community of Practice it is
true that they can also benefit from attention and resources. They can be recognised
and affirmed. They can be connected, one with another as in networks, and they can
be powerful settings for situated learning.

It is important to acknowledge that Communities of Practice and identity formation
are also inseparable. None of us has one singular identity. Each of us responds to the
properties of the given Community of Practice in relation to other memberships. As
Wenger himself puts it:

> We engage in different practices in each of the communities of practice to which we
> belong. We often behave rather differently in each of them, construct different aspects of
> ourselves and gain different perspectives. (Wenger 1999: 159)

Thus the teachers cited in the first example may well be members of other and differently constituted groups such as their professional associations, or their unions. Each of these memberships will also have an influence on how they think and how they conduct themselves.

Communities of Practice, as understood by Wenger, are idiosyncratic. They are developed in context and dependent upon their membership to determine goals and purposes. It would be foolish to imagine that all Communities of Practice are equally effective, purposeful and worthwhile. While they have their place in considering teacher professional learning, they do not have the power and force of more formally constituted Professional Learning Communities.

Forming Professional Learning Communities

As Stoll, Bolam, McMahon, Wallace and Thomas (2006) have noted the formation of professional learning communities hold great promise for capacity building and sustainable school improvement. In their extensive review they adopt Hord's 1997 definition regarding such formations as being those

> in which teachers in a school and its administrators continuously seek and share learning, and act on their learning. The goal of their actions is to enhance their effectiveness as professionals for the students' benefits; thus, this arrangement may also be termed communities of continuous inquiry and improvement. (Hord 1997: 1 in Stoll et al. 2006: 223)

Indeed, we have argued throughout this book that teacher professional learning needs to occur in context and embody opportunities for reflection and critique in the company of others. Capacity building and sustainability are much more likely to occur under these conditions. Fullan (2006: 116) echoes our position when he writes of the power of 'lateral capacity building' across peers as a 'powerful learning strategy'.

Professional Learning Communities then can be seen as deliberate arrangements that bring practitioners together in a systematic way to examine and make problematic features of practice with the intention of development and improvement. The learning is collective, collegial and collaborative. Stoll et al. (2006) believe that effective Professional Learning Communities share five characteristics or features that relate one to another, these being:

- Shared values and vision
- Collective responsibility
- Reflective professional inquiry
- Collaboration and
- Promotion of group as well as individual learning (pp.226–227)

From these it can be taken that an important mediating factor is the capacity of members to articulate and analyse practice. Warren Little (2002) argues that in order to locate teacher learning within a discourse of Professional Learning Communities three central concerns need to be addressed: representations of practice;

orientation to practice; and norms of interaction. She draws upon Wenger's work to suggest that a fundamental problem is 'how the practice of the community comes to be known and shared' (p.934) and suggests that what is vital is that the practice is made visible, transparent and conducted to good purpose in the interests of all who participate. She concludes that if the achievements of Professional Learning Communities are to be seen as significant, then 'we must be able to demonstrate how communities achieve their effects' (p.937). Among other things this suggests the need for participants to take collective responsibility for the community and its work.

While much of the literature in the area suggests that Professional Learning Communities embrace the whole school, it is possible to imagine them as forming for a specific purpose. They are not an end in themselves, but a means of cultivating skills, knowledge and dispositions for specific purposes. To illustrate this we turn to an example where one of us acted as a 'critical friend' to a funded project designed to support early career teachers in a challenging environment in a New South Wales secondary, comprehensive girls' school.

New South Wales is not alone in its concern to retain effective early career teachers in its public schools. Persistent teacher shortages are a significant issue for policy makers from many countries across the world, and it has been indicated that, along with Australia, New Zealand, Canada, the USA and the UK are all experiencing difficulties filling vacancies in their schools. It is argued that problems in teacher supply and demand are both cyclical and complex and it is suggested that such shortages come about when there are particular alignments between demographics, such as an ageing teaching force and policy changes, for example student retention to Year 12, or changes in class size or composition.

It is also clear that the experience of novice teachers mediates whether or not they will stay, or be retained, in their chosen profession. International studies indicate that the transition and adaptation of those beginning to teach can be a harrowing professional journey. Sabar (2004) likened it to the passage of immigrants to a new country. The metaphor is a powerful one in that normally a person does not choose to immigrate alone, but in new teaching appointments may find herself or himself in a strange place experiencing culture shock with little external support. Migration normally involves desires and dreams; similarly, teaching carries the ideals and expectations of the new entrant to the profession.

In the case cited here two early career teachers, one in science and the other in physical education, were placed in a school where a very high proportion of students came from language backgrounds other than English, were Muslim in faith, and often had a general anxiety about school per se. Many were conflicted as they sought to reconcile the values of the wider Australian community and their own Arabic community in particular. In effect, it was a challenging and difficult appointment for teachers new to the profession. They had much to learn.

The school participated in a state-wide programme aimed at retaining new teachers. They were given resources that allowed them to appoint mentor teachers who would support the novice teachers through modelling, observation, discussion and analysis, using a model of practitioner research. The three mentor teachers came from different disciplinary areas, working on the assumption that they would not carry into the observation phase their own beliefs of what constituted 'good practice' for that particular key learning area.

In effect, the novice teachers and their mentors, who worked together for a year, formed a professional learning community within the larger school. It became clear during the course of the project that professional learning was multidimensional. The early career teachers were far more familiar with current pedagogical practices that embraced information and communication technologies; the experienced teachers had a much better informed understanding of the socio-historical context of the school. Knotty problems arose during the study, one being the challenges that were faced when working with para-professionals in the classroom. The novice teachers had not considered what it would be like to engage with teaching assistants who may be much older and more experienced than themselves; the mentor teachers while being familiar in working with aides had not considered their practices in any formal or transparent manner. Each participant in the project was learning in ways that would ultimately not only benefit the early career teachers and their mentors, but also make a contribution to the school's overall policies and practices.

As it happens this brief case arises from the work of the Coalition of Knowledge Building Schools whose practices will form a discrete chapter in this book. It has been cited here as an example of the way in which a professional learning community may not necessarily be inclusive of the whole school, but have an impact across the school nonetheless.

In the portrayal it was indicated that one of the authors of this book was engaged by the school as a 'critical friend'. In their discussion of Professional Learning Communities, Stoll et al. suggest that '[t]here are strong arguments that schools cannot "go it alone" and need connections with outside agencies' (Stoll et al. 2006: 240). In their article they use this claim to move into a discussion of networked learning communities, a matter to which we shall turn shortly. For the moment, though, we believe that it will be productive to discuss the nature and role that can be played by the 'critical friend'.

The Critical Friend: Paradox or Irony

In Chapter 5 we discussed the work of Cochran-Smith and Lytle (2001), who advocate the taking of an inquiry stance. In their writing they assert that '[f]rom an inquiry stance, teachers ... count on other teachers for alternative viewpoints of their work' (p.53). In this sense colleagues are seen as having a capacity to operate as a critical friend within a professional learning community. But what is the critical friend? How can one act in the nurturing, supportive role that is expected from the friend and also have an appraising, challenging, and even confronting disposition? Is the term used paradoxically, or even ironically? There is a tension here. MacBeath and Jardine (1998: 41) see it as 'a successful marrying of unconditional support and unconditional critique', which means that neither trumps the other.

Goodnough (2003) in her self-reflection about her role as a researcher/facilitator of an action research group exploring multiple intelligences theory in the context of science education writes of the need for reciprocity involving mutual recognition and respect. While she was a supporter of the classroom teachers, she was also a challenger. Swaffield (2007: 208–209) explored the role of critical friendship within a multi-site project and outlined a variety of dispositions and activities. The critical friend was involved in liaison, advocacy and engagement as a means of encouraging participation. He or she supported reflection that moved into the realm of questioning and the identification of contradictory and at times conflicting assertions. The study also identified some of the tensions associated with unhappy marriages between the critical friend and the school executive, or where the priorities of the school had changed as a result of other external influences such as school inspections.

In the concluding section of her article Swaffield refers to the English practice of naming a person designated as the school improvement partner as a critical friend who would undertake a conversation with the school in relation to its performance management systems. Thus, we have yet another example of the appropriation of a potentially liberating function, supporting and sustaining teacher inquiry, turning it instead into one that ensures schools are compliant with government requirements. As she concludes:

> [P]resenting schools with a distorted model creates the danger that the concept of critical friendship, a powerful and flexible model of support, will be sullied in the minds of many. (Swaffield 2007: 217)

Elsewhere, writing with John MacBeath, Swaffield concludes that 'governments are prone to cherry picking good ideas and incorporating them into policy initiatives' (Swaffield and MacBeath 2005: 251).

In sum, critical friendship has its own gap – that between the matter of being critical while maintaining a good friendship based upon trust and mutual respect. Just as the subtitle to this book enjoins the reader to 'mind the gap' we too understand the need for caution and care when considering the place of the critical friend in the context of teacher professional learning. We shall return to more fully spell out specific roles that may be played by the critical friend when we present the extended case study of the Coalition of Knowledge Building Schools (CKBS) in the conclusion to this book.

Broadening the Vision: Networked Learning Communities

While Communities of Practice and Professional Learning Communities may be quite modest in scale and self-contained, networked learning communities are generally large organizations. Stott, Jopling and Kilcher (2006: 2) cite a host of collaborative network activities in the UK, the USA, Canada, Germany and Portugal, as well as the iLEARN digital network that operate to improve classrooms and schools across 90 countries. All have in common a desire to contribute to professional learning and to provide conditions where participants can engage in discussion and debate beyond the boundaries of their particular school in ways that are relevant and purposeful. By way of illustration we shall discuss three large learning networks, a little of their history and their orientation; these being The Coalition of Essential Schools (CES) (USA), Networked Learning Communities (UK) and the Australian National Schools Network (ANSN).

Coalition of Essential Schools: Addressing Dialogic Teaching

The Coalition of Essential Schools (CES) was established as a result of its founder's concerns to move beyond a 'good enough' set of compromises regarding how teaching and learning should be conducted (Sizer 1984). Ted Sizer originally established the network with 12 schools; it currently has some 600 formal members. The principles of the network are:

> Learning to use one's mind well
> Less is more, depth over coverage
> Goals apply to all students
> Personalisation
> Student-as-worker, teacher-as-coach
> Demonstration of mastery
> A tone of decency and trust
> Commitment to the entire school
> Resources dedicated to teaching and learning
> Democracy and equity (this principles was added later, in the mid-nineties
> (Coalition of Essential Schools 2006)

Basically, the network is an activist organization taking up a progressive stance in the face of an increasingly conservative education agenda currently in force in the USA. It offers inspiration and resources to its members and has become an important advocate for reform. At the time of its establishment progressive educators were struggling with the Reagan's *A Nation at Risk* policy that sought to standardise and sanitise school practices. Since then, the further entrenchment of national testing (see Chapter 6) has created an environment where such advocacy is seen as critical if transformative education is to continue to flourish.

Networked Learning Communities: Collaborative Enquiry

Networked Learning Communities were established in the UK under the auspices of the National College of School Leadership. Unlike the CES the network was government funded for a specific period of time – 3 years. It was established as a 'research and development programme' (Stott et al. 2006: 2) and provided resources to a total of 109 networked learning communities of at least six schools who had committed themselves to four underpinning principles:

Moral purpose – a commitment to the success of all children
Shared leadership – co-leadership and distributed leadership
Enquiry-based practice – evidence and data-driven learning
Use of a model of learning – systematic engagement with three fields of knowledge (p.3)

As a potential site for teacher professional learning, based upon developing collective solutions to collective problems derived through inquiry, Networked Learning Communities could be seen as liberatory, untrammelled by the kinds of regulatory frameworks that have been so characteristic of school practices in England, Wales and Northern Ireland since the Education Reform Act of 1988. Under the act determinations were made, *inter alia*, regarding the establishment of a national curriculum, key stages and the development of league tables that published the examination results of schools. Networked Learning Communities provided a level of professional autonomy and responsibility. As Stott et al. (2006: 20) observed, 'the networked learning communities programme is distinct amongst Government-funded initiatives, in both its emphasis on learning (professional learning) and the participants' freedom to specify the nature or focus of the activities undertaken to support that learning'.

Nonetheless, the programme has certainly faced some challenges. In spite of many fruitful conversations, study visits and the like, it has emerged that the principle of developing enquiry-based practice has been a difficult one to both maintain and sustain into the future. Networked Learning Communities were required to identify a person who would act as a 'critical friend' and provide challenge and support. Often this person was university-based, although a number of them were also independent consultants or local authority representatives. The role was seen to include:

- Accreditation
- Critical friendship
- Admin research assistance
- Research supervision
- Data collection and analysis
- Project design
- Project monitoring
- Project evaluation
- In-service support/provision
- Co-leadership
- Quality assurance
- Conference organisation
- Financial administration
- Library use

- Specific training
- Demonstrations
- Mentoring
- Finding speakers
- Targeted ITT (Campbell et al. 2005: 46)

Different partners interpreted these roles differently, so for some the support was seen as a means of instructing schools in forms of research that were inimicable to the school's purposes and practices, leading to uncertainty and even acrimony. Partnerships between schools and universities are themselves a matter of some concern when considering various kinds of learning communities. As Seddon, Billett and Clemans (2005: 582) argue:

> Partnerships, their character and consequences are forged at the contested interface between localised networks and central agencies, and they are framed by the broader relations that play through partnerships as well as between partnerships and the wider political order. Like schools, partnerships are sites of struggle. They cannot be dismissed as simple neo-liberal policy instruments.

All the same, the NLC model has been a powerful one and contributed significantly to our understanding of professional learning in the context of practitioner inquiry.

ANSN: Permission to Do Things Differently

The final network to be considered here is the Australian National Schools Network (ANSN) that was established in the 1990s and resulted from an accord between the various state employing authorities and the teachers' unions that moved beyond their industrial role to one that promoted and supported teacher professional learning (Groundwater-Smith 1998). The underlying premise of the partnership was that the conditions under which teachers work are the conditions under which students learn; thus to improve teachers' work and working conditions is to improve student learning. Operating under this rubric it has been possible for schools to step outside some of the normal regulatory boundaries and attempt new and different arrange-ments by varying staffing, school hours and attendance, and teacher to pupil ratios, all of which are normally governed by industrial awards and agreements.

In its own documentation the ANSN stands for a number of principles and offers a number of programmes:

Working together we can achieve more than working alone. That notion under-pins the network's commitment to:

- Improving student learning outcomes
- Rethinking school organisation to improve learning outcomes
- Collaborative and democratic processes
- Active support and promotion of innovative teaching and learning practices
- Bringing about positive changes in schools and schooling

Benefits of joining the network

Members of ANSN can:

- Participate in network projects and research at the leading edge of educational innovation
- Work and share ideas, materials and experience with like-minded professionals – locally, nationally and internationally
- Keep up to date with current developments and future directions
- Access and use sections of the ANSN web site available only to members
- Receive significant discounts on ANSN products and services, such as kits and professional learning activities

Research circles

Members participate in teacher-driven research work, designed around questions of interest to schools. Groups of schools collaborate nationally, testing the relevance of innovative ideas in their own work contexts. Based on the results of this work, members produce materials and develop professional learning opportunities for other educators – within and beyond the network.

Professional learning

The network designs and delivers high-quality professional learning activities, where participants think and work 'outside the square'. These include workshops, seminars, courses, forums and school-based work on improving professional practice, often related to network projects and research. Activities can be tailored to suit school, district or system needs. Recent training programmes and workshops have included work in the following areas.

- Protocols to look at student work
- Cognitive coaching
- Leading for learning
- Team/small group training
- Interactive whiteboards in action learning and the classroom
- Restorative justice
- Action learning and action research
- Assessment by exhibition
- Authentic learning and digital portfolios
- Early childhood and technology
- Engaging with habits of mind
- Interactive whiteboards in the classroom
- Restorative justice
- Numeracy across the curriculum (Australian National Schools Network)

In recent years the network has been less generously funded than in the past and it is now incumbent upon its members to pay for its various services. Nonetheless, it continues as a powerful force in supplying resources for teacher professional learning and providing opportunities for teachers from different schools, systems and states to encounter and learn from each other.

Conclusion

In returning to our initial reference to 'knots' we now connect this powerful metaphor to the discussions and examples that we have outlined above. Engestrom (Engestrom et al. 1999) who first identified the concept of organisational 'knots' and 'knotworking' argues that no single actor has sole, fixed, line-managed, bureaucratic authority, but the work is based upon what he designates as 'co-configuration' whereby there is continuing interaction between those who engage in developing, designing and delivering services and those who are the end-users (Engestrom, 2004). He sees co-configuration as dialogic requiring ongoing interaction that is interpretive and negotiated and involves all key stakeholders. It is a difficult, demanding and ambiguous work. He quotes one who has sought to operate in this way:

> The actors are like blind players who come eagerly to the field in the middle of the game, attracted by shouting voices, not knowing who else are there and what the game is all about. There is no referee, so rules are made up in different parts of the field among those who happen to bump into one another. Some get tired and go home. (Engestrom 2004:13)

Perhaps, at times, teachers can be a little weary of the constraints that are heaped upon them. It is our belief that if we are to fully support teacher learning through inquiry, then the various forms of learning community outlined in this chapter have the greatest potential for unravelling some of those things that can inhibit and restrain them.

Part IV
Closing the Gap

Chapter 10
Case Study: The Higher Degree

Doctoral pedagogy is as much about the production of identity,
then, as it is the production of knowledge.

(Green 2005: 162, emphasis in original)

Having laid out our understanding of inquiry-based professional learning, from its historical roots to its essential qualities to the current tensions, contradictions and competing agendas in undertaking inquiry-based professional learning in today's age, in this chapter and the one which follows, we present two case studies of inquiry-based professional learning in action – one individual case, relating to the undertaking of a higher degree; and one systemic case, relating to the work developed within a school network configured around the taking of an inquiry approach.

In this chapter, Nicole (one of us) presents the story of her own doctoral study as a 'case' demonstrative of the capacity of the research degree to function as inquiry-based professional learning. It has been written as a first-person narrative, and as such represents a discursive shift from earlier chapters, which in turn represented a discursive shift themselves from the prior task of authoring a Ph.D. thesis.

The Case

As I come to write this case, the examiners' reports on my thesis have just arrived, and the reality that this chapter in the journey is finally finished has scarcely had time to hit. In the 3 months since my thesis was submitted, I have begun to gain something of a holistic perspective on the doctoral experience, although I guess that this reflection will gain more clarity over the coming months when the degree will be conferred and I get used to the idea that it is indeed over. I have structured this reflection into three parts which represent what for me were distinct elements of the process: the stroll in, the endurance race through and the sprint out. My doctoral research saw me working with a number of teachers to develop life history narratives from which an understanding of professional identity could be 'mined' (Mockler 2008), and I have used a similar approach in the construction of this, my own biographical narrative.

S. Groundwater-Smith and N. Mockler, *Teacher Professional Learning*
in an Age of Compliance, DOI: 10.1007/978-1-4020-9417-0_10,
© Springer Science + Business Media B.V. 2009

Getting In

When I think carefully about it, I have probably aspired to 'do' a Ph.D. for about half my life. As an undergraduate student, I studied a Bachelor of Education (Secondary – English and History) with Honours in Ancient History at the University of Sydney, and then in my first 2 years of teaching completed an MA in History and Gender Studies. The intention had always been to one day return to study for a higher degree in History – for me, this was driven by a desire to sustain my attention on a project that would be life-giving as well as life-defining, over a number of years and, in the words of a participant in Leonard et al.'s study of the benefits of doctoral study: 'To prove myself at the highest level. To pursue a set of ideas to their logical conclusion' (Leonard et al. 2005). As I went through the process of becoming a teacher; however, education took hold, and at the same time, watching a number of friends who had taken a bumpy ride through very long and torrid Ph.D. studies in Ancient History struggle to find a place within the academy where they would be supported and formed as researchers, the allure of History faded somewhat. Encouraged by a principal for whom I worked for a number of years, and who was most encouraging of my educational and leadership capacities, to study towards a Master of Education, I began to extend my knowledge of educational theory, and found increasingly that my day-to-day practice was reflexively informed by my learning at university, particularly in terms of curriculum design, educational leadership and change.

At the time, the school I was working in was embarking on major and whole-school change, and I was fortunate to have the opportunity to play (an informal) leadership role within the development and implementation of this change. Upon becoming a Head of Department at the beginning of my fifth year of teaching, I became increasingly aware of the ongoing reflexive relationship between my studies and my practice as a school leader as well as a teacher, and became progressively more interested in the interplay of theory and practice not only within my own experience as an educator but also within the experience of those teachers for whom I had formal leadership responsibility, as well as my colleagues and indeed school more broadly. I was supported in this emerging understanding by the school's Director of Teaching and Learning (DoTL), an outstanding educational leader with a big vision for education and professional learning, an excellent role model in terms of leadership and a person with a strong commitment to mentoring and supporting Heads of Department such that they were formed as leaders and agents of change within the school.

It was at this point and through the leadership of the DoTL that I became engaged in my first inquiry-based professional learning experience. Furthermore, the DoTL organised for Susan (co-author of this book) to engage in the project as academic partner, and thus began in embryonic form what has been a most creative and fruitful working relationship. Emerging from the initial practitioner research project and having had my 'eyes opened' to authentic and powerful professional learning for the first time in my career, I continued on to engage with the DoTL and other colleagues in subsequent practitioner inquiry initiatives, both funded and unfunded, and was encouraged strongly by Susan to convert my in-progress Master of Education into a professional doctorate, utilising some of the practice-based research skills I had developed.

Encouraged particularly by my principal and the DoTL to seek promotion in my third year as Head of Department, I found myself embarking on a big new job as Director of Learning in a different school, and simultaneously, or at least one term later, embarking on my Doctor of Education (EdD) coursework. This was a time of both great excitement and a steep learning curve for me. At the age of 29, I was the youngest member of both the Heads of Department team (of which I was Chair and 'The Boss') and the school's Leadership Team, by about 20 years. Most teachers my age within the school were considered to be little more than beginning teachers, and yet I was charged with the task of leading learning, large-scale pedagogic and curriculum change and also managing the 'nitty gritty' of curriculum administration, feeling pressure all the while to demonstrate my skills, knowledge and pedagogical capabilities, and in doing so constantly justifying my position within the school. I brought with me, learned through my apprenticeship with the DoTL, a firm belief in the importance of good, differentiated teacher professional learning as the primary, if not the only, effective catalyst for educational change, and within that a commitment to inquiry-based professional learning. Much of the work done by myself and others within the school in this regard was documented over the next 5 years in conference papers and journal articles (Mockler 2000, 2001, 2002, 2003; Groundwater-Smith and Mockler 2001, 2002, 2003a; Mockler and Sachs 2002).

Getting Through

I began my doctoral studies supervisor-less, with a vague idea of a focus on practitioner inquiry as professional development. By the conclusion, 8 years from the outset of the original EdD coursework, the degree itself had morphed from an EdD to a Ph.D., my work had transformed twice – after 3 years as the Director of Learning my role within the school had become so large that the Principal determined to 'split' it into Professional Learning and Student Learning roles, with the role of Director of Professional Learning developed specifically for me around my skills and capacities, as well, of course, the needs of the school and the teachers within it. Then, 3 years subsequent to taking on the new role as the school's internal professional development consultant, I embarked upon my own independent education consultancy. Meanwhile, the thesis itself, in terms of both focus and methodology, had been through several radically different iterations, with the final one established about a year before submission.

The first catalyst came during the first year of EdD coursework, when I returned to my 'old' school to hear the academic who was to become my supervisor, speak about teacher professionalism. I had met her a couple of years previously when, as the new professor within my faculty, she had taken a class I was in for a few weeks while the lecturer was overseas. Although I knew she had a formidable intellect, I did not realise that our areas of interest were so similar until I heard her speak, and afterwards I found myself approaching her, egged on by my ex-principal, with whom I had been seated, to ask if she would consider taking me on as a student. We organised to meet and I must have said something mildly impressive (or at least not made a complete goose of myself), because she agreed to be my supervisor and set me to work at that point on my literature review.

Over the course of the next year, my reading took me from practitioner research to professional development more broadly and then to the centrality of teacher identity, and it was here that I arrived by the time I submitted my thesis proposal, 2 years later. The proposal was deemed by both my supervisor and the faculty to be more appropriate for a Ph.D. thesis than an EdD, due to its strong theoretical framework and intention to make a theoretical contribution. While the focus of my research remained quite static (in general terms, at least) from that time forward, the methodology went through a number of iterations, spurred on by some catalysts I shall elaborate upon.

At this time, the school I was working in as Director of Professional Learning was going through a major reinvention, at the heart of which was a reorientation towards what is often referred to as 'twenty-first century learning', contextualised within a commitment to social justice and transformation. Additionally, the spiritual and religious tradition in which the school was located lent great emphasis to the notion of 'formation', in the sense of 'becoming' for teachers, and I found myself increasingly spending time with teachers working to build their confidence in their own capacities, helping them to identify the gaps in their knowledge and understanding of pedagogy and learning and finding interesting ways to fill those gaps, and as best I could, removing the 'roadblocks' that stood in the way of the provision of the kind of education that as a school we had decided we wanted to offer. It was at a time when teachers had been bombarded for about a decade with 'new' ideas about pedagogy and learning – differentiation of the curriculum, learning styles, authentic assessment, multiple intelligences, autonomous learning, information literacy, student-directed learning, negotiated curriculum, constructivism, online learning and so on and so forth.

I arrived thus at a focus on teacher professional identity not only out of my reading and thinking about teacher professional development, but also out of my day-to-day work with teachers and an emerging understanding that it is not only what teachers know and can do that impacts upon the way they do their work and engage with their students, but also *how they see and position themselves*: in relation to students, education, knowledge and each other. While this understanding of professional identity was very much built on the work done by my supervisor and others in relation to profession-wide professional identity, my intention was to look at the formation and impact of professional identity on a local level. The original plan was to work with teachers from three schools, conduct a range of focus groups, develop a survey utilising qualitative and quantitative methods for distribution to teachers in 12 schools and write up the results.

The process of gaining ethics approval, both from the University's Human Research Ethics Committee and from the New South Wales Department of Education and Training, was a fairly arduous one which took approximately 6 months and added little to the process other than to develop my understanding of the enormous divide between the worlds of scientific/medical research and qualitative research in the social sciences. This was despite the entreaties of Gorman (2007) for human research ethics committees to work in partnership with researchers, seeking to enrich the quality of research. Nevertheless, 6 months later I began to enlist schools (a process which was more difficult than I had anticipated it to be) and headed off into the field to collect my data.

The second catalyst came in the form of an epistemological break (less in the Althusserian sense than the psychotic sense) that made me rethink my approach in a most fundamental way. At the end of 2004, I had given up my 'real job' and set up my education consultancy, frustrated with my lack of progress on my Ph.D. study and aiming to spend some sustained time finishing the data collection (at this stage I had been working with only one of the three 'case study' schools) and writing. Working in a reflexive way with my growing theoretical understanding of professional identity, my own professional identity was undergoing radical transformation: for the first time in my professional life I was not part of a school community, not working alongside children in a sustained way, not in any kind of formal, recognised 'leadership' role. The impact of this experience fed into my growing understanding of how professional identity is both formative and yet also subject to changes in the professional landscape.

About 6 months into the following year, my research was still 'limping' along, partly because of the amount of work I had managed to generate but more importantly because of my growing sense that in terms of the emerging understanding of identity that I was still developing out of both my reading and my work with teachers in a variety of contexts, that perhaps I was not going about the study in the right kind of way. The break came after I attended a session at the Sydney Writers' Festival on an Australian Research Council-funded Linkage Project known as *The Thesis to Book Project*. The project, which was a collaboration between the University of Sydney and the publishing house PanMacmillan, awarded a Post-Doctoral Fellowship to a recent Ph.D. graduate each year for 3 years, providing them with mentoring from Drusilla Modjeska, an Adjunct Professor at the University and arguably Australia's finest literary non-fiction author. The session at the Writers' Festival involved Drusilla, one of the Fellows, a Ph.D. in Philosophy called Justine McGill and the Publisher, in discussion of the project, including quite an in-depth discussion of Justine's thesis and its elements that gave it such great promise in terms of becoming a work that might be published as a literary non-fiction book and make something of a difference to society at large.

I still do not really know how it happened but somehow the seminar gave me the space that I needed to think for a short while about what it was that I wanted to do in my own thesis, and how I might best go about understanding professional identity. I emerged from the session with some clarity about the importance of history in the emergence of teacher professional identity and proceeded over the coming months to research the processes of educational life history and to reconfigure my research plans, ethics approval and so on. The more I learned about life history research and read studies that employed this methodology in an educational context, the more confident I became that this would provide me with answers to (some of) my questions about teacher professional identity, and ultimately lead me to write the kind of elegant, scholarly and downright interesting thesis that I desired to author. I moved initially to an approach that would conduct life history interviews with four case study teachers and then a survey with a much larger group to, 12 months later, having learned an enormous amount about the conduct and processes of this kind of work as well as having become quite entranced by the very 'thick' data I was collecting, an entire life history approach with a second quartet of teachers and a broad-based analysis of teachers in public discourse which could be brought into dialogue with the eight biographical narratives.

With a friend and fellow doctoral student I piloted each 'round' of interviews and was fortunate to receive frank and fearless feedback, as well as hours of discussion about the very notion of teacher professional identity as it played out in our lives as teachers and teacher educators. Here I honed my interview technique (although the bulk of my development as an interviewer, a journey far from as yet complete, happened throughout the course of the study) and found an honest 'critical friend' in robust discussion of my theorising as it developed.

Getting Out

By October 2007, I had collected most of my data and had written a draft version of every chapter with the exception of the final two. The biographical narratives I had developed out of the interview data were well received by participants and despite my dreams of 'co-construction' not being realised there, I was confident in the knowledge that my participants felt that I had 'made sense' of their professional lives in a way that 'made sense' to them. Interestingly, the only moments of angst concerning the biographical narratives related not to their *content*, but rather to the extracts from interview transcripts, where two of the participants worried that they sounded either foolish or uneducated (or both). This was very easily amended to our mutual satisfaction but has given me food for thought regarding the process of interview within critical research, and will continue to do so for some time to come.

So having emerged on the 'other side', where am I now? The first thing that strikes me is that this process has provided me with a stark reminder of how much I *do not* know. Far from the ideal of the independent researcher elaborated in the literature on doctoral research (Gardner 2008), I feel at this point more like a neophyte than I possibly ever have. Furthermore, I have become quite bemused since submitting my thesis at the disconnect between the perception of the Ph.D. outside the academy, where it connotes a certain cleverness, and bestows 'expert' status, and within it, where it functions as a kind of membership card and 'provisional driver's licence. This disconnect leaves me feeling somewhat bifurcated as I move between these two worlds.

What the process of completing my doctoral study has done for me is to encourage me to see my practice and that of the teachers with whom I have worked through the lenses of both practice *and* theory (although I would also challenge this very dichotomy). While my doctorate was not in the end a 'professional doctorate', for me it was intimately and reflexively linked to the various contexts of my work over the 8 years it was completed, such that when I look at it now I can hardly see where the influence of research on practice stops and the influence of practice on research begins. In this, I think that it goes some way towards challenging the notion that doctorates relating to professional practice in some ways cannot help but 'buy into' regimes of efficiency and effectiveness (Lee et al. 2000). In very practical ways, I know that my understanding of the formation of professional identity has made me infinitely more patient with the teachers with whom I work, more understanding of the complex links between self and professional practice and more conscious of the importance of helping teachers to articulate the links between what they do and why they do it.

As both a doctoral graduand and a scholar of identity, I concur with Green's assessment, reproduced at the outset of this chapter, that doctoral scholarship is as much about the production of identity as the production of knowledge. A key finding from my doctoral work itself was around the notion of 'identity anchors' - those events, experiences or exposures that occur in either personal, professional or external political domains which form and re-form identity (Mockler 2008). Even at this close distance I can observe in myself this particular anchor taking hold, throwing up identities I am more or less comfortable with at this stage of my professional life – that of 'researcher' I may take a little longer than this to feel I have earned; that of 'expert' I hope I might always eschew; and that of scholar-teacher I feel I have been flirting with for some years now but may actually have made an advance on.

Conclusion

This case has served to illustrate the ways in which even that which might be regarded as a more 'theoretical' than professional higher degree can be influenced by, and in turn influence, professional practice, thus constituting an example of inquiry-based professional learning. In this case, the professional learning undertaken related not only to the student's development as a researcher (although this was indeed significant in itself) but also to her broader field of professional practice, leading her to grapple with some of the key and persistent issues she identified within the field. The constant and highly reflexive relationship between the field of practice and the research process itself over an extended period saw both dimensions impacted upon, and changed by, the other.

The higher degree as an example of inquiry-based professional learning provides a new set of insights into the critical issues discussed at length in Chapter 8, namely those of purpose, process, outcome and ethics. For while the higher degree is largely free of the constraints and compliance requirements of much state-funded action or practitioner research, a different set of constraints and compliance issues prevails by virtue of the field of the academy within which this research takes place. While the research agenda and processes employed, for example, are generally determined by the researcher in an autonomous fashion (albeit in consultation with the research supervisor), and, as in the case reported above, are often subject to considerable shifts according to the researcher's experience on the way 'through', the constraints and 'red tape' placed upon researchers within the social sciences by virtue of ethics processes which are tailored specifically to deal with scientific and medical research bring their own compliance agendas to the table. In the context of a research project which has a critical bent, such as that reported in the case above, the determination that the research will contribute to a broader political initiative, and that the processes will be implemented transparently with a concern not only for the researcher but also for the participants, responds to some of our concerns regarding evidence and process. While it falls short of our 'collaborative' requirement (in the vast majority of cases and most certainly in the one reported here), the requirement that the research justify itself to the academic community of practice is demonstrated in the processes whereby the student works under the guidance of a research supervisor and also in the submission of the final product to a number of external evaluators, as well as, in many contexts, the 'defence' process.

It is possibly in terms of the issues of action and effect, relating to the outcomes and consequences of the research, that the higher degree can potentially depart from the ideals of inquiry-based professional learning. The thesis is often seen as an end in itself, whereas the transformative dimension of inquiry-based professional learning requires that there are active consequences and outcomes from the research process which work to make conditions better for students and teachers. In the example of the case outlined above, these outcomes are yet a 'work in progress', although the findings from the research and the research process itself will continue to inform the practice of the researcher in her work with teachers in schools over the years to come.

Having considered an individual case in the instance of study towards a higher degree, we move now to consider a larger-scale systemic example of inquiry-based professional learning with which we have both been engaged.

Chapter 11
The Coalition of Knowledge Building Schools

In the first of his 2006 Reith Lectures, on the interplay between music and society, Daniel Barenboim argued that in order to make music in concert with others we have to learn to listen to what others are playing. His point was that in a society dominated by individualism there is a need to return to a more enduring and generous collectivism. This can only be achieved when each is prepared to listen and attend to others. School education in many ways mirrors the concerns raised by one of the world's great conductors, individualism is still the dominant professional mode (Elmore 2000). Teachers work alone in classrooms; schools work in isolation from one another. Universities and schools occupy parallel universes and never the twain shall meet. (Groundwater-Smith 2006a: 1)

This chapter reports upon the Coalition of Knowledge Building Schools (CKBS) established in Sydney, Australia, a decade ago. Working in conjunction with the Centre for Practitioner Research at the University of Sydney, members of the Coalition go about their work examining current practices and investigating new possibilities. Members share problems and prospects and have developed new methodologies for practitioner inquiry. The chapter will report upon the ways in which these transactions occur through the lens of several case studies as well as subsequent publications, and the contribution that these make to professional knowledge formation.

A particular emphasis in the chapter will be on the nature of knowledge formation in the current educational context which can be simultaneously seen as a place where schools market themselves, but where there is also a marketplace for ideas. It will explore the development of educational and educative knowledge that is crafted by those who well understand the purpose to which it is to be put as a form of Mode 3 Knowledge growing from the concept of Mode 2 Knowledge (Gibbons et al. 1994), as we discussed in Chapter 4. Such knowledge production is concerned with the identification and solution of practical problems in the lived professional lives of practitioners and organisations not encircled by the boundaries of a single discipline. The chapter will illustrate, through the case studies and subsequent publications, the ways in which these boundaries are becoming more interesting and problematic.

Australia has a long history of network formation between schools, albeit in small pockets. For many years, across Australia, federally funded equity programmes such as the former Disadvantaged Schools Program[1] (DSP) brought schools facing

---

[1] Currently rebadged in New South Wales as the Priority Schools Funding Program (PFSP).

S. Groundwater-Smith and N. Mockler, *Teacher Professional Learning in an Age of Compliance*, DOI: 10.1007/978-1-4020-9417-0_11, © Springer Science+Business Media B.V. 2009

similar challenges in given regions to work collaboratively on curriculum resources and teaching and learning strategies. However, in recent years, programme funding has increasingly been tied to narrowly defined federal government policy objectives with fewer opportunities for schools to work on broadly based, locally derived, responsive, cooperative ventures. Although there are some notable exceptions, in particular 'The Fair Go Project' (Munns, Zammit and Woodward 2006), which is an ongoing study into student engagement among low-socio-economic status (SES) students in primary schools in Sydney's south-west. It is a joint undertaking between university-based researchers, New South Wales (NSW) Department of Education and Training officers, teachers and community members. It aims to assist in the development of a pedagogy that results in substantive engagement in high-cognitive, high-affective, and high-operative classroom processes and experiences, and embrace students as 'insiders in their classroom learning communities'.

In Chapter 9 we discussed two examples of school-to-school networks that also involved university partners. At the beginning of the 1990s the *Innovative Links for Professional Development Between Schools and Universities Project* was also formed across all but one of Australia's states and territories. This involved 14 Australian universities working with small networks of schools to investigate matters of local concern (Groundwater-Smith 1998). Similarly, the National Schools Network (NSN) which burgeoned during the 1990s was established at this time. The NSN operated upon the basis that the conditions under which teachers worked were also the conditions under which their students learned; thus, the industrial and professional agenda were seen to intersect. The Innovative Links Project has long gone while the NSN now exists only as a shadow of its former self. One must ask oneself why these effective and educative networks have not lasted. Partly, it can be argued that both the Innovative Links Project and the NSN were developed in an environment in which there was a period of industrial settlement – that is where there were agreements between employing authorities, unions and professional associations to curb wage demands and work cooperatively. It was through the instrument of 'The Accord', as it became known, that both of these projects were born. The overarching wages and income accord jointly signed by the Australian Labor Party and the Australian Council of Trade Unions was to last from 1983 to 1996 when it met its demise following the election of the Liberal National Coalition Government (Kuhn 2002). Networking based upon across-the-board agreements of this kind would become a thing of the past. Although, under a new more conciliatory government they may well become, once more, a thing of the future.

So what is it that encourages us to believe that forming and maintaining networks can be a powerful agency for educational reform and development, for teacher professional learning? And can networks themselves learn?

Networks – A Strategy for Reform

In writing of schools as intelligent organisations MacGilchrist et al. (2004) have recognised that there is a professional intelligence that goes beyond that of the individual. There is what they have named a collegial intelligence 'that enables the core functions of a school and their related technologies to be articulated, developed, transported and used' (p.134). They assert that the resultant knowledge creation is produced not by individuals alone, but as a result of the school working as an organic whole.

How then can we characterise networks in general, and The Coalition of Knowledge Building Schools as a network in particular, and why argue that they themselves are an intelligent response to contemporary conditions of professional practice when they can be so fragile and easily dispensed with, or when they can be riddled with knots, as suggested in Chapter 9?

Chapman and Aspin (2005: 10) have defined networks thus:

> Networks are intentional constructions, linking together in a web of common purposes. They are self-conscious and deliberately established organic entities in which all the constituent elements are equal in the weight of enmeshment that they carry and the responsibility that they bear for making contributions towards the whole.

They believe that network integration needs to work both horizontally and vertically and to engage multiple stakeholders. Levin (2004) has argued that much mandated reform in the public sector has not worked well. Partly this is attributable to the unidirectional nature of the intended reform with little or no consultation with those who will most bear the costs and consequences. Thus, inclusive networks as a strategy for reform have a certain appeal. They would seem to have the capacity to bring a number of different elements and players together into some kind of coherence. However, as Stoll (2005) has noted, networked learning communities are a means to an end; they are not an end in themselves. They have a capacity to 'move ideas and good practice around the system, helping transform the whole system, not just individual schools' (p.36). Of course this goal is only realisable in a context where cooperation transcends competition.

As to the capacity for networks to learn, we have to ask ourselves whether there is evidence of growth and change. Are there collective learning outcomes? Is what is known, known collectively, albeit with different and multiple perspectives? Is there 'transparency, receptive capacity, reciprocity, social depth, trust, a long term outlook, learning together and from each others, cultural compatibility, similarity of vision, a body of expertise and "double framing?"', all of which are seen by Keka'le and Viitala (2003: 245) as key indicators of a capacity for networks to learn.

In today's world, it has been argued, organisations such as schools have to learn constantly in order to respond to an ever-changing environment and to remain competitive, for there can be no question that schools themselves are in a marketplace. But, as has been argued elsewhere, that marketplace is not only one where education is a commodity to be traded like any other, but also one where ideas can be circulated, discussed and defended (Groundwater-Smith 2006b). Such is the case with The Coalition of Knowledge Building Schools.

The Coalition of Knowledge Building Schools

Let us return for one moment to Daniel Barenboim's argument that in order to make music in concert with others we have to learn to listen to what others are playing and extend the metaphor slightly. If the Coalition of Essential Schools discussed in Chapter 9 could be characterised as symphony orchestra and The English Networked Learning Communities as operatic in scale, then the Coalition of Knowledge Building Schools might better be seen as a small, but demanding, chamber music ensemble – modest in size but committed to complexity and excellence. The work of the Coalition has been well documented (Groundwater-Smith and Mockler 2003a; Groundwater-Smith and Dadds 2004). In brief, it is a network of 13 schools that now extends beyond the Sydney Metropolitan Area to include regional schools and one that can be said to be rural and remote. Also it counts among its members extended learning organisations such as the local zoo education centre and Australia's largest and oldest museum. The network has been built gradually, beginning as it did with only three Independent Girls' Schools, each of which undertook a funded action research project within various federal government programmes during the late 1990s. Through the initiative of Sydney University's Centre for Practitioner Research[2] the schools began meeting each other to informally discuss their projects, the methodologies that they were employing and the outcomes that they had achieved. Gradually other schools, including government schools facing the most demanding and challenging circumstances, came to join the group. They too had initially been involved in small funded projects. As time went by the group determined to develop a more formal brief for themselves, as follows:

- To develop and enhance the notion of evidence-based practice[3]
- To develop an interactive community of practice using appropriate technologies
- To make a contribution to a broader professional knowledge base with respect to educational practice
- To build research capability within their own and each other's schools by engaging both teachers and students in the research processes and
- To share methodologies which are appropriate to practitioner inquiry as a means of transforming teacher professional learning (Groundwater-Smith and Mockler 2003b: 1)

What is important to note is that the Coalition continues to grow and flourish largely outside the funding arena. A number of the schools have committed their own internal professional learning funds to various projects. However, it should be recognised that the synergy of the group also contributes to its members being successful in bids for various grants. It is also notable that the network welcomes opportunities to contribute to wider projects that provide benefit to the greater community and which may not attract any funding. For example, over the past several years schools have participated in various Australian Museum consultations, bringing the perspectives of young people to the attention of curators and designers

---

[2] Now renamed The Practitioner Research Special Interest Group in the Faculty of Education and Social Work.

[3] This term is one that the Coalition has embraced in its broadest sense, believing it to mean evidence that is gathered in a forensic rather than adversarial sense (Groundwater-Smith and Dadds 2004).

(Groundwater-Smith and Kelly 2003; Groundwater-Smith 2006c). The network itself is unfunded, thus being accountable only to its members. If it did not meet its members' needs it would cease to exist. Costs to individual schools relate to the release of teachers to the three meetings per year and a final 1-day conference aimed at enhancing the professional learning of all, including the academic partners who give freely of their time but who also benefit, professionally, from their ongoing contact with schools engaged in innovation and change.

One such example is in relation to teacher feedback during the annual conference conducted by the Coalition. At the end of 2006, teachers from all participating schools were asked to contribute to an academic paper focusing upon the nature of teacher professional learning (Sachs 2007). They posted notes on their vision of teaching in the twenty-first century and the kinds of continuing professional learning that was needed to inform that teaching. As one teacher put it:

> [We need] to be flexible to the ever changing environment, including society, technology and the world in which we live. We often find ourselves in different positions, sometimes moulding to these positions and other times needing greater flexibility of training. (Sachs 2007: 1)

Another identified the kind of training and development that was found to be unhelpful and limiting:

> [The worst kind of continuing professional development] is unintellectual – anything redolent of the worst kind of pop psychology, jargon filled with no explanations, 8.00 am to 3.00 pm at the local club for one day, a wonder session by a visiting guru. Boys are from Mars, left brain, right brain, multiple intelligences cross hatched with Blooms taxonomy. (Sachs 2007: 4)

As Sachs noted, this group of teachers who have worked with each other, across schools, for a sustained period of time know what they want and need in terms of their professional learning: they want to be challenged; they want to share their practices and work with colleagues; and they want opportunities to re-examine their beliefs and practices. We would add, from our experience, that they want to do these things in an environment governed by mutual trust and an openness of spirit.

In order to illustrate the work of Coalition Schools we shall offer two case studies. It must be emphasised that each one of the 13 member schools is actively engaged in one form of inquiry or another. The cases have been selected on the basis of being developed in two very different socio-economic circumstances and designed to meet different purposes. However, each has employed methodologies that have been developed by the Coalition as a whole.

Case 1 – Differentiating Boys' Learning in Years 7 and 8

Inner City Boys High School has been an active member of the Coalition of Knowledge Building Schools for the past 7 years. During that time it has undertaken a number of reviews of practice as well as specific interventions. It is currently engaged in a Lighthouse Project, 'Success for Boys'. It is a school that values evidence-based practice, reaching back into the 1990s when it was a foundation member of the National Schools Network and participated, among other things, in the now defunct Innovative Links Project. It was also a school in receipt of the former Disadvantaged Schools Program funding that necessarily involved it in collaborative planning and innovation.

The school has been operating with teaching teams for Years 7 and 8 over more than a decade and has been seen as a model for middle years education. However, during this time much has changed in the school's demographics, its teaching staff, and the structure of secondary schooling in Sydney's inner city. A *Building the Future* initiative resulted in the formation of new clusters of schools, including senior high school, and dedicated streams for gifted and talented students. One such cluster has been developed within the same drawing area as Inner City Boys High School. Also there are other specialised schools in the area including selective secondary schools for high-achieving students. All this means that the school has to work hard in the educational marketplace to attract students whose parents would like them to participate in a boys' education programme that caters for the full range of ability, including those who are most able.

There are now more boys of South-east Asian origin attending the school, and some of them are in the school on a full-fee-paying basis. This is a new trend in Australian school education, particularly in the government sector. Overseas students contribute significant funds towards the school budget, but also involve additional responsibilities for the school. The school is no longer a grantee within the Priority Schools Funding Program, the successor to the Disadvantaged Schools Program.

While the team structure has continued for Years 7 and 8, several other changes have occurred. Using Australian Council of Educational Research (ACER) tests, which identified the abilities of Year 6 students in preparation for making the transition to secondary school, an extension class was established for the most able students with remaining students placed in three parallel classes. In catering for the more able boys, the school has also been cognisant of special needs that students may have. There is a Learning Support Unit that assists in the integration of students into the remaining three parallel classes.

Clearly a range of provisions that can assist, to some extent, in differentiating or personalising learning are in play for Years 7 and 8. Not all of these provisions are seen as positive by a number of members of staff, who have a stronger inclination towards overall comprehensive schooling.

Given these many arrangements in a context of an ever-changing educational environment and a previous history of evaluating its policies and practices it was thought to be opportune to again cast an eye on Years 7 and 8, in particular the arrangements made for differentiating the education of boys in these middle years.

The Inquiry

In the context of a review of the relevant research on the provision of gifted and talented education, personalised learning and the educational needs of boys, the study explored the existing perceptions of strategies being used to meet the varying needs of boys in Years 7 and 8 that are held by students and staff and parents. It employed both focus group methodology and a survey approach.

A discussion paper on boys' educational needs in the middle years was developed and circulated. The Coalition has a strong orientation to gathering evidence not only from practices within the participating schools, but also from the wider research field. It has been argued that the position paper can be a useful tool for:

- Clarifying thinking about a proposed change or possible pathway
- Drawing together current research findings and theoretical perspectives in order to better inform decision-making
- Fuelling professional discourse around significant issues and
- Challenging cherished beliefs and understandings (Groundwater-Smith and Mockler 2003b: 25)

The paper contributed to a healthy debate within the school regarding *which* boys and *what* needs.

Senior boys were trained to conduct focus groups with younger boys and undertook and documented these. Again this is a strategy that has been well developed in the Coalition. From the reported results a student questionnaire was developed and analysed, in turn, by a senior computing class.

Focus groups and individual interviews with teachers were undertaken and a questionnaire developed and administered. A parent forum took place later in the year where parents were advised of the inquiry results and provided with opportunities to respond to them.

The research has been managed by an in-house team and facilitated through the work of the previously mentioned Practitioner Research Special Interest Group from the University. The costs of the research have been met by the school. The case study can be seen as an illustration of the way in which a Coalition member has undertaken a local inquiry. Recalling Keka'le and Viitala's indicators of network learning the inquiry demonstrated transparency, reciprocity and social depth, trust, a long-term outlook, and learning together and from each others in that the school shared its inquiry and findings with their colleagues in the Coalition. These indicators can also be seen to be apparent in the case that follows.

Case 2 – A Learning Laboratory in an Activist School

Independent Girls' School is a relatively wealthy, faith-based school. It caters for students from Kindergarten to Year 12 and is notable for its ongoing innovative responsiveness to student needs. It is a foundation member of the Coalition and has been supportive of it in a number of material ways including making a financial contribution to the publication of the widely adopted resource *Learning to Listen: Listening to Learn* (Groundwater-Smith and Mockler 2003b).

The school is divided into three sub-schools: junior, middle and senior. Year 9 is the first year of senior school and one that is not subject to any statewide testing or high-stakes assessment. For some it is seen as a year where students mark time.

At Independent Girls' School it is seen as a year where students may be engaged in new and different regimes and activities. It is a school where one of us has played the role of Researcher in Residence, a role that has been undertaken over a number of years.

The Year 9 Laboratory has a number of components, among them: a prolonged stay in a remote location where students employ a range of information and communication technologies to undertake their studies of the local environment, a year-long independent investigation in relation to a question of concern to the individual student, and longer blocks of learning time and changing places and spaces for learning. Also, arrangements for academic care have changed.

During the first year of the Year 9 Laboratory it was seen as essential that it would be one where there would be a formative evaluation that would not only document developments, but would also provide a number of benchmarks for ongoing improvement. In this case two research groups were formed. The external research group comprised an educational psychologist, an information and communication technology (ICT) academic and a teacher educator from the area of mathematics education. The internal research group included the Year 9 coordinator, the head of senior school, a science educator, and the Director of Studies. The researcher in residence was a member of both groups as was the school principal. While the groups met individually, they also met as a combined group once each term. Also, the inquiry had two reference groups, one comprised of student representatives, and the other of parents. Following reference group meetings deliberations were published on the school's Intranet for the wider community of students, parents and teachers.

The Inquiry

During the year a number of different inquiry procedures were undertaken. There exist multiple measures of student engagement and motivation that can be set against internationally derived norms, and these were employed. Again, focus groups were used as a significant tool. In this case, some new procedures were trialled such as the use of music as a stimulus and ice-breaker for the groups. Some shadowing of students was undertaken as was participant observation in relation to the different spaces and places for learning. The internal research group established a protocol, *Making Learning Visible*, for collecting information upon a sample of students as they progressed through the year. In all cases informed consent was sought and granted.

This study is one that required considerable resources which the school committed as part of its overall planning for ongoing development. In common with other schools in the Coalition there was also a commitment to publish the study, not only to fellow members, but also to the wider research community. Members of the school staff participated in a presentation focusing upon the employment of multi-methods in a single case to the Australian Association for Research in Education later that year (Groundwater-Smith et al. 2006). This paper will be discussed more fully later in this chapter.

In common with other schools in the Coalition, Independent Girls' School also presented at the 1-day conference to be conducted by the Coalition for its members at the end of this year.

These two cases, abbreviated as they are, serve to provide some substantiation for the claim that the Coalition of Knowledge Building Schools is a network that fosters the development of professional knowledge and supports the capacity of its members to engage in productive and useful inquiry. There is clearly an important connection between innovation and networked learning. However, we cannot be too sanguine for there are some pitfalls and traps that lie not far under the surface of even this successful group.

The Knowledge Marketplace – Problems and Prospects

In the beginning of this chapter it was claimed that it would explore the development of educational and educative knowledge that is crafted by those who well understand the purpose to which it is to be put as a form of Mode 2/3 Knowledge (Gibbons et al. 1994). Such knowledge production is concerned with the identification and solution of practical problems in the lived professional lives of practitioners and organisations not encircled by the boundaries of a single discipline. We would argue that the Coalition of Knowledge Building Schools has indeed been engaged in developing such knowledge, making an important contribution to the knowledge marketplace.

It is important to recognise that while the Coalition is not in receipt of external funding, it nevertheless would be inoperable if participating schools did not contribute teachers' time and resources to the work. Furthermore, it is dependent upon the goodwill and energy of those who convene the group and support it with expertise. The Practitioner Research Special Interest Group in the Faculty of Education and Social Work at the University of Sydney is itself unfunded. It is supported by three academic members who act as honoraries – in other words, their commitment to the Special Interest Group and the work of the Coalition is dependent upon their goodwill. Certainly, each may be engaged, from time to time, as a paid consultant to a particular project undertaken by a given school. However, the matter of convening and maintaining the group and writing of its considerable achievements counts for little in the academy (Groundwater-Smith and Mockler 2006).

There are significant opportunity costs for all who participate. Busy school-based practitioners must find time beyond their classroom commitments to their students to gather, analyse, interpret and act upon various inquiries. University practitioners wishing to operate as 'close-to-practice' teacher educators are aware of the lack of recognition that is given to their work. Seemingly, though the benefits must exceed these costs for such a robust association to endure. We now turn to the ways in which the Coalition has made a wider contribution to debates and discourses regarding teacher professional learning.

Publishing to the World and the Village

In Chapter 2 it was argued that on the one hand the dissemination of research into school education is too often published to the world rather than the village. That is, scholarly papers are produced in the form of refereed journal articles or conference proceedings that are unlikely to be read and acted upon within the schools themselves. On the other hand, that which is published for the village, particularly through professional associations and the like, is neither recognised nor rewarded by the academy. We would claim that the work of the Coalition is somewhat unusual in that it seeks to contribute to debate and discussion both locally and globally.

We have referred a number of times to the resource *Learning to Listen: Listening to Learn* (Groundwater-Smith and Mockler 2003b). At the time of its publication one of us was leading professional learning in a Coalition school and was able to contribute to the discussion from a practitioner's perspective. The document was the result of a joint venture between another of the participating schools and the university. All schools who were members at that time contributed examples from their practice and were able to review and edit the resource, which has been purchased by both schools and higher education institutions in Australia and overseas. We see this as an important contribution to the development of practice as it is constructed by members of the Coalition.

Returning for a moment to the paper cited in the second case study in this chapter (Groundwater-Smith et al. 2006), its contribution lay not only in reporting upon the innovation but also upon the nature of employing multiple methods both qualitative and quantitative. Creswell (2003) has argued for the employment of mixed methods as a process where the researcher collects, analyses and integrates both qualitative and quantitative data in a single study in ways that may be concurrent, sequential, conversion or parallel. Merten (2003) has proposed that mixed methods have a significant potential for informing emancipatory and transformative practices. For the purposes of the study, in-house and external researchers saw that the various components of the study were both concurrent and interactive. In effect, they established what Katerndahl and Crabtree (2006: 443) have termed a 'methodological think-tank': an approach that uses team-building concepts to develop quickly a shared common space for identifying innovative ways of integrating quantitative and qualitative methods to study important but challenging research questions – in this case, the nature of the processes, procedures and outcomes of the Year 9 Learning Laboratory.

In addition to this presentation several Coalition members made a determination to report on their work to an international conference, the joint Collaborative Action Research Network (CARN)/Practitioner Research Conference held in the Netherlands in 2006. Two papers were presented. Needham's (2006) paper reported upon the school's experience in engaging students as partners in inquiry, while Mockler et al.'s (2006) paper explored practitioner research as a catalyst for the improvement of student learning in given and particular contexts alongside the development of transformational, ethical teacher professionalism. All papers were subject to refereeing scrutiny prior to the conference.

Other members of the Coalition have been successful in publishing in refereed journals, having been enabled by the collective in establishing and refining their ideas. Elliott (2008: 57) outlined an approach to lesson study in the form of master classes. He was careful to assert that 'master classes are really for teacher-learners, not for master-teachers'. The process was an adaptation of the well-regarded lesson study approach where teachers planned, enacted and analysed the ways in which they teach what may be regarded as challenging concepts. In Elliott's case the approach was adapted so that experienced practitioners, who were the 'pioneers' in opening up their practices for wider scrutiny and professional conversation, would initiate teaching/learning episodes that would allow the observation of student learning, engagement and motivation. In his article he focused upon the developmental process that was adopted and some of the difficulties that were faced, thus making a significant contribution to the wider discussions regarding teacher professional learning. The approach adopted by Elliott was first mooted at a Coalition day conference in which participants provided feedback and advice.

Conclusion

Singh (2007) in his introduction to his discussion of the provision of a sound research base for teacher education quotes Raymond Williams (1983: 248, 240) when he argued that 'professional research is an "actual and immediately potential resource" for "making hope practical, rather than despair convincing"' (p.333). Throughout this book we have questioned the compromises that have to be made when the press to compliance is at its greatest. The kind of research that can be undertaken within a Mode 2/3 knowledge economy, such as has been described in this chapter in terms of the work of the Coalition of Knowledge Building Schools, leads us to 'making hope practical', for all who participate in it are afforded a space in which to participate with an authentic and realised sense of agency and where the network itself is seen as a complex, professional organism that can also learn.

Effectively it learns as an intelligent organisation that has a capacity to reflect, to question and to disseminate. We earlier cited the work of MacGilchrist et al. (2004), who propose that there are many intelligences that govern the ways in which organisations can function maximally to the benefit of those who participate in them. Among them are intelligences governing ethical behaviour, contextual understanding, operational capacity, emotional awareness, collegiality, and deep pedagogical insight. Just as we hope that learners in our schools have opportunities to exercise the many intelligences that they possess, so too do we have high expectations that the Coalition can continue to grow and flourish.

Chapter 12
Closing the Gap: Conclusion

> *I think it only makes sense to seek out and identify structures of authority, hierarchy, and domination in every aspect of life, and to challenge them; unless a justification for them can be given, they are illegitimate, and should be dismantled, to increase the scope of human freedom. - Noam Chomsky, in an interview conducted by Kevin Doyle in the Red and Black Revolution.*

(May 1995)

While it should not be taken that this book is a call to revolution, or indeed some kind of anarchic epistle in relation to teacher professional learning we do share a perspective with Noam Chomsky that it is right to identify the structures of authority, power and control that limits the possibility of developing professional practice as that which is moral and good. Throughout this book we have sought to argue that much of what passes for provisions to enhance professional learning are procedures designed to create an uncritical and compliant work force able to be bent to the political will.

We began the book with four problematics, which, understood as current orthodoxies, might be seen to pose a threat to progressive education and authentic, generative professional learning. They were:

- The rise of audit cultures
- Standardisation of practice
- The diminishment of teacher professional judgement and
- The 'quality' agenda in education

Together, these problematics represented for us the dangers posed to education by the compliance agenda, and throughout the preceding 11 chapters we have attempted to pose a counterpoint to the tyranny of compliance by suggesting that should these orthodoxies be allowed to uncritically and unquestioningly guide the educational agenda into the next decade, we risk an impoverishment of both professional practice and education itself.

S. Groundwater-Smith and N. Mockler, *Teacher Professional Learning in an Age of Compliance*, DOI: 10.1007/978-1-4020-9417-0_12, © Springer Science+Business Media B.V. 2009

In this concluding chapter we wish to draw together some threads that are fundamental to closing the gap between the aspirations of those who would have teachers
as functionaries and those whose desire is for teachers to transcend compliance and
work towards transformational practices designed to 'make hope practical' as discussed
at the conclusion of Chapter 11. To this end we wish to assert that the progressive
notions of practice for which we are advocates are precarious in today's fiercely
global society; that as one solution is generated it brings us face to face with new
problems and new prospects; that we need to build resilience into professional practice
as a means of strengthening the resolve to resist the more limiting impositions
placed upon it, to consider what might constitute a 'health check' for the profession
and to reflect upon what kinds of buffers might be put in place that will increase the
scope of professional freedom.

The Precarious Nature of Progressive Educational Practice

On a sociological level, the human response to uncertainty and complexity is well
documented: the more tenuous and complex it becomes 'out there', the more humans
tend to seek stability and 'answers' (Giddens 1990; Castells 1997; Apple 2006). In the
globalised world, dominated by uncertainty of all kinds and reflected in the growth
of knowledge economies, the rise of fundamentalism and terrorism and the current and
impending effects of climate change, control and standardisation can look appealing.
Within the education arena, we see this manifest in 'common-sense' approaches that
prize the standardisation of practice, standardisation of student assessment and the
proliferation of 'what works' across diverse contexts and circumstances. Like motherhood, it is hard to argue with 'quality', and while such practices remain camouflaged
in 'improvement' and the camouflage itself remains uncontested, it is likely that such
practices will remain. Only through developing resilience as a profession and
mobilising our professional judgement in forums that count are we likely to provide
a counter strategy that will 'stick'. Furthermore, we contend that it is only through
courageous action and a willingness to be countercultural in the face of 'common
sense' on the part of teachers and teacher educators that the 'gap' will be closed.
    Our emphasis here has been to focus upon inquiry-based professional learning as
both an enabler and fosterer of such professional judgement and professional courage.
High-quality practitioner inquiry has the potential not only to build these in teachers
who engage, but also to provide careful and precise local solutions to local issues and
concerns, pushing through the 'one-size-fits-all' orthodoxy of compliance cultures.

Moral Authority and Moral Agency

Throughout this book we have insisted upon teachers' right to behave morally, in
relation to both their students and their profession. (AS Ax et al. 2008) observe:

> [T]eachers and school leaders are being deprived of their 'moral agency' and their inclination and ability 'to do the right thing'. ... Educators risk getting caught in a system compelling them to follow rules and behave instrumentally. ... The challenging thesis is, that teachers should act 'educationally' which means that they should demonstrate practical wisdom. (p.250)

'Wisdom' seldom appears in the contemporary education lexicon. However, we contend that the teacher who acts wisely does so in the interests of not only their individual students, but also in the broader interest of human well-being. It may be in the interest of one student to allocate them disproportionate attention and resources because they demonstrate a high level of intellectual capacity, but it may not be in the interest of their peers. The wise teacher and the wise system have a responsibility to balance the needs of each and determine a just and fair outcome.

Our emphasis has been upon the teacher as 'good citizen' exercising their rights and responsibilities that are too easily violated by the press to compliance. Cherie Booth in writing in the Guardian newspaper (2006) quoted Eleanor Roosevelt as one of the architects of the UN Charter of Human Rights, saying that human rights 'begin in small places close to home' and that unless rights have meaning in our neighbourhoods, schools and workplaces, 'they have little meaning anywhere'. Remembering that our schools are not only places for student and teacher learning, but also teachers' workplaces, the message is both powerful and poignant.

Our Chosen Voice

One means of closing the gap is a choice that we have made, as authors and constructors of this text, to employ a language that we believe is not only accessible, but also stripped of the bureaucratic and distancing vocabulary that excludes the practitioner from the kind of deep engagement that we are advocating. We are mindful of the kind of style so often adopted to obscure the meaning of the text and to marginalise the reader. George Orwell, in his contentious essay 'Politics and the English Language' (1946) argued thus:

> The inflated style is itself a kind of euphemism. A mass of Latin words falls upon the facts like soft snow, blurring the outlines and covering up all the details. The great enemy of clear language is insincerity. When there is a gap between one's real and one's declared aims, one turns, as it were instinctively to long words and exhausted idioms, like a cuttlefish squirting out ink. (p.6)

In addition to eschewing 'weasel words', in this work we have also aimed to question some of the more established 'bureauspeak' in its educational usage. In our approach to discussing 'quality', 'standards' and 'community', for example, we have aimed to push through the common usage to examine what these terms *really* mean, both as 'markers' and in educational practice.

Furthermore, we have consciously adopted different 'voices' for different purposes within the text, employing, for example, a more personal voice in the case study chapters, where we report upon our own work and experience more directly than in other chapters.

Complex Solutions for Complex Problems

We suggested in Chapter 1 that one of the hallmarks of the current age is the tendency to propose simple, 'common-sense' solutions to what are in fact complex, multidimensional and often situational problems. The courage and resilience required to live with ambiguity, to resist the urge to develop and then replicate simple 'solutions' across multiple and diverse sites, and indeed to scrutinise such 'out-of-the-box' solutions when they are provided by governments and systems is a critical part of closing the gap. Claiming and defending the necessarily complex landscape of education and promoting an understanding of the human dimension of all aspects of the education enterprise is a key task for the profession at this time - doing so effectively will ensure that the impoverished notions of education which guide some of the key current policy directions across the Western world will not remain unexamined and uncritiqued.

There is a prevailing sentiment that defines social, economic and political issues as those that can be resolved through management alone. 'Efficiency' is the clarion cry with a plethora of edicts emerging from government regarding standards and measures of performance. Thus, decisions regarding the ways in which teachers may exercise their professional judgement in response to increasingly complex problems are constrained by increasingly simplistic solutions.

Professional Judgement and Professional Freedom

The teaching profession is currently at a crossroads. As we discussed in Chapter 1, hand in hand with the intensification of teachers' work over the past 15 years has come an unwillingness to trust what is seen as the 'subjectivity' or teacher professional judgement in favour of more 'objective' measures such as standardised testing and other forms of competitive assessment. If the human dimension of education is to be acknowledged and valued, the reclaiming of teacher professional judgement as a trusted and respected tool, developed through and based upon reflection on and in professional knowledge and practice, is critical. Understanding that teacher professional judgement is more than a random grab bag of 'ideas' and 'feelings' based upon casual and formal interactions with students and other stakeholders is a significant element of this reclaiming, and this part of the gap will only be closed when the current orthodoxy of objectivity and standardisation is questioned and critiqued in the public forum.

This process of reclaiming teacher professional judgement must start with the profession itself, finding voice within schools and professional associations in particular, and sending a consistent message to governments and bureaucracies that poses a challenge to the furphy of objectivity and standardisation. The first step in this process lies in redeveloping the professional confidence of teachers such that they feel capable and knowledgeable in their capacity to engage in such debates, and for us inquiry-based professional learning provides a pathway to the building of such confidence.

Conclusion

The neo-liberal economic and social agenda has had a pervasive impact upon education across the developed world. Strategies which arguably make good economic sense and provide governments with laudable 'evidence' of 'educational improvement' do not always translate into real improvements for students, or contribute to the realisation of the broader transformative goals of education. We have argued throughout this book that professional learning, which is inquiry-based, rigorous, engaging and concerned with maximising learning for both teachers and students, holds the potential to do both. Five years ago, Sachs concluded her book *The Activist Teaching Profession* with a call to action for educators to become the 'kind of profession that can educate our children to be socially active and responsible citizens', claiming that 'there is no time to lose' (2003b: 154). Similarly, Michael Apple concluded his critique of conservative and fundamentalist approaches to education in *Educating the Right Way* with a call to educators to use hope as a practical and critical resource in proactively countering the orthodoxies of our time (Apple 2006: 261–262). We believe that if anything, the landscape of educational policy has become more enamoured of agendas which work against this vision rather than for it in recent years.

We thus conclude with our own call to action-for the teaching profession itself as well as those who serve it, such as teacher educators-to pose a challenge to the compliance agenda in education in all its manifestations. Such a challenge is not likely to be easy, swimming as it is against the tides of compliance, instrumentalism, fundamentalism and neo-liberalism which so categorise the contemporary age. Given what is at stake, however, we can scarcely afford not to work vigorously and strategically to close the gap between contemporary policy and practice and truly generative and transformative education.

References

Ahmed, P. & Machold, S. (2004). The Quality and Ethics Connection: Towards Virtuous Organisations. *Total Quality Management,* 15 (4) pp. 527–545.

Alexander, B. (2006). Web 2.0: A new wave of innovation for teaching and learning? *Educause Review,* March/April, pp. 33–44.

Aspin, D. et al. (2005). *International Perspectives on Networked Learning.* Nottingham: National College of School Leadership.

Apple, M.W. (1986). *Teachers and Texts: A Political Economy of Class and Gender Relations in Education.* New York: Routledge.

Apple, M.W. (2000). *Official Knowledge: Democratic Education in a Conservative Age.* New York: Routledge. (2nd Edition).

Apple, M.W. (2006). *Educating the 'Right' Way: Markets, Standards, God and Inequality.* New York: Routledge Falmer. (2nd Edition).

Arnot, M. & Reay, D. (2007) A Sociology of Pedagogic Voice. *Discourse,* 28 (3) pp. 311– 326.

Atkinson, E. (2004). "Thinking Outside the Box: An Exercise in Heresy." *Qualitative Inquiry* 10(1): 111–129.

Australian College of Educators (2008). *Quality Teaching Awards 2008: Learning Form and Recognising our Best Teachers.* Sydney: DET and ACE. Available from http://www.austcolled. com.auindex.phpoption=com_content&task=view&id=2172&Itemid=523, Accessed 20 April 2008.

Australian National Schools Network http://www.ansn.edu.au/about accessed 29th May, 2008.

Ax. J. Ponte, P. Matteson, M. & Ronnerman, K. (2008). Reflections on Enabling Praxis. In S. Kemmis & T. Smith (Eds.) *Enabling Praxis.* Rotterdam: Sense Publishers, pp. 243–262.

Ballet, K., Kelchtermans, G. & Loughran, J. (2006). Beyond intensification towards a scholarship of practice: analyzing changes in teachers' work lives. *Teachers and Teaching: theory and practice.* 12 (2) pp. 209–229.

Bernstein, B. (2000). *Pedagogy, symbolic control and identity: Theory, research and critique.* (Rev.Ed.) Lanham, MD: Rowman and Littlefield.

Berthoff, A. (1987). "The Teacher as REsearcher", in *Reclaiming the Classroom: Teacher Research as an Agency for Change.* D. Goswami and P.R. Stillman (Ed.). New Jersey: Boynton/Cook. pp. 75–86.

Bland, D. & Atweh, B. (2007). Students as researchers: engaging students' voices in PAR. *Educational Action Research* 15 (3) pp. 337–349.

Booth, C. (2006). How to be a good citizen. *The Guardian* Tuesday, September 12th.

Borko, H. (2004). 'Professional Development and Teacher Learning: Mapping the Terrain'. *Educational Researcher,* 33 (8), pp. 3–15.

Bryk, A. & Schneider, B. (2002). *Trust in Schools: A Core Resource for Improvement.* New York: Russell Sage Foundation.

Burke, C. & Grosvenor, I. (2003). *The School I'd Like: Children and Young People's Reflections on an Education in the 21ˢᵗ Century.* London: Routledge Falmer.

Campbell, A., Keating, I., Kane, I., McConnell, A. & Baxter, C. (2005). *Networked Learning Communities and Higher Education Links.* Nottingham: National College of School Leadership.

Caro-Bruce, C., Flessner, R., et al., Eds. (2007). *Creating Equitable Classrooms through Action Research.* Thousand Oaks: Corwin Press.

Caro-Bruce, C. and Klehr, M. (2007). Classroom Action Research with a Focus on Equity. *Creating Equitable Classrooms through Action Research* C. Caro-Bruce, R. Flessner et al. Thousand Oaks: Corwin Press.

Carr, W. and Kemmis, S. (1986). *Becoming Critical: Education, Knowledge and Action Research.* London: Falmer Press.

Carroll, L. (1946). *Alice's Adventures in Wonderland.* London: Penguin Classics (original published 1865).

Castells, M. (1997). *The Power of Identity.* Massachusetts: Blackwell.

Castells, M. (2001). Local and Global: Cities in the Network Society. *Tijdschrift voor Economische en Sociale Geografie*, 93 (5) pp. 548–558.

Chapman, D. & Aspin, D. (2005). Why Networks and Why Now? In D. Aspin et al. *International Perspectives on Networked Learning.* Nottingham: National College of School Leadership. Pp. 10–14.

Clark, A. (2008). *History's Children*, Sydney: University of New South Wales Press.

Clarke, J. and Newman, J. (1997). *The Managerial State.* Thousand Oaks, CA: Sage Publications.

Clarke, C. & Rumbold, K. (2006). *Reading for Pleasure: A Research Overview.* London: National Literacy Trust.

Coalition of Essential Schools. (2006). *Ten Common Principles.* http://www.essentialschools.org/pub/ces_docs/about/phil/10cps/10cps.html. Accessed 28 May 2008.

Coccari, D. (2007). We Want to Work With Our Friends. *Creating Equitable Classrooms through Action Research* C. Caro-Bruce, R. Flessner et al. Thousand Oaks: Corwin Press.

Cochran-Smith, M. (2003). "The Unforgiving Complexity of Teaching: Avoiding Simplicity in the Age of Accountability." *Journal of Teacher Education* **54**(1): 3–5.

Cochran-Smith, M. and Lytle, S. (1990). "Research on Teaching and Teacher Research: The Issues that Divide." *Educational Researcher* **19**(2): 2–11.

Cochran-Smith, M. and Lytle, S. (1992). "Communities for teacher research: fringe or forefront?" *American Journal of Education* **100**: 298–324.

Cochran-Smith, M. and Lytle, S. (1993). *Inside/Outside: Teacher Research and Knowledge.* New York: Columbia University Teachers' College.

Cochran-Smith, M. and Lytle, S. (1998). "Teacher research: the question that persists." *International Journal of Leadership in Education* **1**: 19–36.

Cochran-Smith, M. and Lytle, S. (1999). "Relationships of Knowledge and Practice: Teacher Learning in Communities." *Review of Research in Education* **24**: 249–305.

Cochran-Smith, M. & Lytle, S. (2001). Beyond Certainty: taking an inquiry stance on practice. In A. Lieberman & L. Miller (Eds) *Teachers Caught in the Action: Professional Development that Matters.* New York: Teachers College Press.

Cochran-Smith, M. and Lytle, S. (2007). "Everything's Ethics: Practitioner Inquiry and University Culture", in *An Ethical Approach to Practitioner Research: Dealing with Issues and Dilemmas.* Campbell, A. and Groundwater-Smith, S. (Ed.). London: Routledge.

Colucci, E. (2007). "Focus Groups Can be Fun": The Use of Activity Oriented Questions in Focus Group Discussions. *Qualitative Health Research* 17 (10) pp. 1422–1433.

Connell, R. (2007). Teachers. In R. Connell, C. Campbell, M. Vickers, A. Welch, D. Foley & N. Bagnall. *Education, Change and Society.* Oxford: Oxford University Press, pp. 262–278.

Corey, S. (1953). *Action Research to Improve School Practices.* New York: Teachers College Press.

Cornu, B. (2004). Networking and collective intelligence for teachers and learners. In A. Brown & N. Davis (Eds) *Digital Technology, Communities and Education.* London: Routledge Falmer, pp. 40–45.

Creswell, J. (2003). *Research Design: Qualitative, Quantitative and Mixed Methods Approaches.* Thousand Oaks, CA: Sage Publications.

Dadds, M. (1993). "The Feeling of Thinking in Professional Self-study." *Educational Action Research* **1**(2): 287–304.

Dadds, M. and Hart, S. (2001). *Doing Practitioner Research Differently*. London: Falmer Routledge.

Darling-Hammond, L. (1996). "The Right to Learn and the Advancement of Teaching: Research, Policy and Practice for Democratic Education." *Educational Researcher* **25**(6): 5–17.

Darling-Hammond, L. (1997). *The Right to Learn: A Blueprint for Creating Schools that Work*. San Francisco: Jossey Bass.

Darling-Hammond, L. (1999). *Reshaping Teaching Policy, Preparation and Practice: Influences on the National Board for Teaching Professional Standards*. Washington, DC: AACTE Publications.

Darling Hammond, L. (2006) Securing the Right to Learn: Policy and Practice for Powerful Teaching and Learning. *Educational Researcher* 35 (7) pp 13–24.

DEST (2001). *School Innovation: Pathway to the Knowledge Society*. Canberra: DEST.

Dewey, J. (1904). *The Relation of Theory to Practice in Education: The Third NSSE Year Book*. Chicago: University of Chicago Press.

Dewey, J. (1916). *Democracy and Education*. New York: The Macmillan Company.

DfES (2004). *Working together: Giving children and young people a say*. Department for education and skills. London: The Stationary Office.

Donnelly, K. (2004). *Why Our Schools are Failing*. Sydney: Duffy & Snellgrove.

Education Guardian (2006). Teachers Prioritising Targets Over Study Skills Research Shows. *Education Guardian*, August 9th, 2006.

Elliott, G. (2008). Master Classes: building on the 'lesson study' approach in an Australian School. *Teacher Leadership*, 1 (3) pp. 48–58.

Elliott, J. (1997). "School-based curriculum development and action research", in *International action research: A casebook for educational reform*. S. Hollingsworth (Ed.). London: Falmer.

Elmore, R. (2000). *Building a New Structure for School Leadership*. Washington, DC: Albert Shanker Institute.

Engestrom, Y., Engestrom, R. & Vahaaho, T. (1999). When the center does not hold: the importance of knotworking. In S. Chaiklin, M. Hedegaard and U. Jensen (Eds) *Activity Theory and Social Practice*. Aarhus: Aarhus University Press.

Engestrom, Y. (2004). New forms of learning in co-configuration work. *Journal of Workplace Learning* 16 (1/2) pp. 11–21.

Eraut, M. (1994). *Developing Professional Knowledge and Competence*. London: Falmer Press

Eraut, M. & Hirsh (2007). *The Significance of Workplace Learning for Individuals, Groups and Organisations*. Oxford and Cardiff Universities ESRC Centre on Skills, Knowledge and Organisational Performance.

Facer, K., Furlong, J., Furlong, R. & Sutherland, R. (2003). *Screenplay: Children and Computing at Home*. London: Routledge.

Fenstermacher, G. (1994). "The knower and the known: the nature of knowledge in research on teaching." *Review of Research in Education* **20**: 3–56.

Fenwick, T. (2007). Organisational learning in the 'knots': Discursive capacities emerging in a school-university collaboration. *Journal of Educational Administration* 45 (2) pp. 138–153.

Fielding, M. (2004a). "New Wave Student Voice and the Renewal of Civic Society." *London Review of Education* **2**(3): 197–217.

Fielding, M. (2004b). Transformative approaches to student voice: theoretical underpinnings, recalcitrant realities. *British Educational Research Journal*, 30 (2) pp. 295–311.

Fielding, M. (2007). "Beyond Voice: New Roles, relation and Contexts in Researching with Young People." *Discourse: Studies in the Cultural Politics of Education*. **28**(3): 301–310.

Fielding, M., Elliott, J., Burton, C., Robinson, C. & Samuels, J. (2007) *Less is More? The Development of a Schools-within-Schools Approach to Education on a Human Scale*. Centre of Educational Innovation, University of Sussex.

Fine, M. (1992). *Disruptive Voices*, NY: University of Michigan Press.

Foster, P. (1999). "Never Mind the Quality, Feel the Impact: A Methodological Assessment of Teacher Research Sponsored by the Teacher Training Agency." *British Journal of Educational Studies* **47**(4): 380–398.

Freiesleben, J. & Pohl, T. (2004). Quality: An Ethical Inquiry. *Total Quality Management*, 15 (9/10) pp. 1209–1216.

Fullan, M. (1993). *Change Forces: Probing the Depths of Educational Reform*. London: Falmer.

Fullan, M. (2001). *Leading in a Culture of Change*. San Francisco: Jossey Bass.

Fullan, M. (2006). The future of educational change: system thinkers in action. *Journal of Educational Change*, 7 pp. 113–122.

Fullan, M. (2007). *The New Meaning of Educational Change*. New York: Teachers' College, Columbia University. 4th Edition.

Furlong, J. & Oancea, A. (2008). Expressions of Excellence and the Assessment of APPlied and Practice-Based Research. In J. Furlong & A. Oancea (Eds.) *Assessing Quality in Applied and Practice-Based Research in Education–Continuing the Debate*. London: Routledge pp 1–19.

Gardner, K. (2008). ""What's Too Much and What's Too Little?": The Process of Becoming an Independent Researcher in Doctoral Education." *Journal of Higher Education* **79**(3): 326–351.

Garet, M. S., Porter, A. C., et al. (2001). "What Makes Professional Development Effective? Results from a National Sample of Teachers." *American Educational Research Journal* **38**(4): 915–945.

Garrett, P. (2007). "New England and New Labour: Retracing American Templates for the Change for Children Programme?" *Journal of Comparative Social Welfare* **23**(1): 31–47.

Geertz, C. (1983). *The Way we Think Now: Towards an Ethnography of Modern Thought*. New York: Basic Books.

Gibbons, M., Limoges, C., Nowotny, H., Schwartzman, S., Scott, P. & Trow, M. (1994). *The New Production of Knowledge: The Dynamics of Science in Research in Contemporary Societies*. London: Sage.

Giddens, A. (1977). *Studies in Social and Political Theory*. New York: Basic Books.

Giddens, A. (1990). *The Consequences of Modernity*. Cambridge: Polity.

Giddens, A. (1998). *The Third Way: The Renewal of Social Democracy*. Cambridge: Polity Press.

Giddens, A. (2002). *Runaway World: How Globalisation is Reshaping our Lives*. London: Profile.

Gillborn, D. & Youdell, D. (2000). *Rationing Education*. Buckingham: Open University Press.

Goodnough, K. (2003). Facilitating action research in the context of science education: reflections of a university researcher. *Educational Action Research*, 11 (1) pp. 41–63.

Goodson, I. (1993). "The Devil's Bargain: Educational Research and the Teacher." *Education Policy Analysis Archives* **1**(3).

Goodson, I. (1997). "'Trendy Theory' and Teacher Professionalism", in *Beyond Educational Reform: Bringing Teachers Back In*. A. Hargreaves, Evans, R. (Ed.). Philadelphia: Open University Press. pp. 29–43.

Gorman, S. (2007). "Managing Research Ethics: A Head-on Collision?" in A. Campbell and S. Groundwater-Smith (Eds), *An Ethical Approach to Practitioner Research*. London and New York: Routledge.

Goswami, D. and Stillman, P.R. (1987). *Reclaiming the Classroom: Teacher Research as an Agency for Change*. New Jersey: Boynton/Cook.

Green, B. (2005). "Unfinished Business: Subjectivity and Supervision." *Higher Education REsearch and Development* **24**(2): 151–163.

Green, H. & Hannon, C. (2006). *Their Space. Education for a Digital Foundation*. London: DEMOS Foundation.

Greenfield, P. (1996). Culture as process. In J. Berry, Y. Poortinga & J. Pandey (Eds.) *Handbook of Cross Cultural Psychology Vol. 1 (Revised Edition)* Needham Heights: Allyn & Bacon, pp. 301–346.

Grosvenor, I. & Burke, C. (2008). *School*. London: Reacktion Books.

Groundwater-Smith, S. (1998). "Putting teacher professional judgement to work." *Educational Action Research* **6**(1): 21–37.

Groundwater-Smith, S. (2006a). The Coalition of Knowledge Building Schools: A market place for developing and sharing educational practice. Paper presented to the British Educational Research Association Annual Conference, Warwick, September.

Groundwater-Smith, S. (2006b). Professional Knowledge Formation in the Australian Market Place: Changing the Perspective. *Scottish Educational Review*, 37 (Special Edition – Teacher Education and Professional Development) pp. 124–131.

Groundwater-Smith, S. (2006c). Millennials in Museums: Consulting Australian Adolescents when Designing for Learning. Invitational Address presented to the Museum Directors' Forum, National Museum of History, Taipei, 21st–22nd October, 2006.

Groundwater-Smith, S. & Dadds, M. (2004). Critical Practitioner Inquiry: Towards Responsible Professional Communities of Practice. In C. Day & J. Sachs *International Handbook on the Continuing Professional Development of Teachers*. Maidenhead: Open University Press, pp. 238–263.

Groundwater-Smith, S. & Kelly, L. (2003). Through Our Eyes: Learning in the Museum. Paper resented to the European Conference on Educational Research, Hamburg, 17th–20th September.

Groundwater-Smith, S., Martin, A. Hayes, M., Herrett, M., Layhe, K., Layman, A. & Saurine, J. (2006). What Counts as Evidence: Mixed Methods in a Single Case. Paper presented at the AARE Annual Conference Adelaide, 26th–30th November 2006.

Groundwater-Smith, S., Mitchell, J. & Mockler, N. (2007). *Learning in the Middle Years: More than a Transition*. Melbourne: Thomson.

Groundwater-Smith, S. and Mockler, N. (2001). "The Knowledge-Building School: From the Outside In, From the Inside Out." *Change: Transformations in Education* 5(2): 15–24.

Groundwater-Smith, S. and Mockler, N. (2002). *Building Knowledge, Building Professionalism: The Coalition of Knowledge Building Schools and Teacher Professionalism*. Paper presented to the AARE Annual Conference, University of Queensland, St Lucia, December 2002.

Groundwater-Smith, S. and Mockler, N. (2003a). *Holding a Mirror to Professional Learning*. Paper presented to the Annual Conference of the Australian Association for Research in Education and the New Zealand Association for Research in Education, Auckland, NZ, December 2003.

Groundwater-Smith, S. & Mockler, N. (2003b). *Learning to Listen: Listening to Learn*. Sydney: MLC School & Faculty of Education, University of Sydney.

Groundwater-Smith, S. & Mockler, N. (2006). Research that counts: practitioner research and the academy. In J. Blackmore, J. Wright & V. Harwood (Eds) *Review of Australian Research in Education*, RARE 6, pp. 105–118.

Groundwater-Smith, S. and Mockler, N. (2008). "Ethics in Practitioner Research: An Issue of Quality", in J. Furlong and A. Oancea (Eds), *Assessing Quality in Applied and Practice-Based Research in Education: Continuing the Debate*. Abingdon and New York: Routledge.

Groundwater-Smith, S. & Nicoll, V. (1980). *Evaluation in the Primary School*. Sydney: Ian Novak.

Grundy, S. (1982). "Three modes of action research." *Curriculum Perspectives* 2(3): 23–34.

Grundy, S. (1995). *Action Research as Professional Development*. Murdoch, WA: Innovative Links Project.

Gutmann, A. & Thompson, D. (1996). *Democracy and Disagreement*. Cambridge, Mass: The Belknap Press of Harvard.

Halpin, D. (2003). *Hope and Education: The Role of the Utopian Imagination*. London: Habermas, J. (1987). *Theory of Communicative Action, Volume 2: System and Lifeworld: The Critique of Functionalist Reason*. Boston: Beacon.

Hansen, D. (1994). Revitalizing the Idea of Vocation in Teaching. Accessed on 27 January 2008 from http://www.ed.uiuc.edu/EPS/PEs-Yearbook/94_docs/HANSEN.HTM.

Hardy, I. and Lingard, B. (2008). "Teacher Professional Development as an Effect of Policy and Practice: A Bourdieuian Analysis." *Journal of Education Policy* 23(1): 63–80.

Hargreaves, D. (1996). *Teaching as a Research Based Profession*. London: Teacher Training Agency.

Hargreaves, D. (1999). "The knowledge-creating school." *British Journal of Educational Studies* **47**(2): 122–144.

Hattie, J. (2003). *Teachers Make a Difference: What is the Research Evidence?* Melbourne: Australian Council for Educational Research. Available from http://www.acer.edu.au/documents/ RC2003_Hattie_TeachersMakeADifference.pdf, Accessed 20 April 2008.

Hazlett, S., McAdam, R. & Murray, L. (2007). From Quality Management to Socially Responsible Organisations: The Case for Corporate Social Responsibility. *International Journal of Quality and Reliability Management,* 24 (7) pp. 669–682.

Hodkinson, P. (2004). Research as a form of work: expertise, community and methodological objectivity. *British Educational Research Journal,* 30 (1) pp. 9–26.

Hollingsworth, S. (1994). "Feminist Pedagogy in the Research Class: an example of teacher research." *Educational Action Research* **2**(1): 49–70.

Hollingsworth, S. (1997). "Killing the Angel in Academe: Feminist Praxis in Action Research." *Educational Action Research* **5**(3): 483–500.

Hollingsworth, S. & Gallego, M. (2007). Editorial Team's Introduction: Special Issue on No Child Left Behind. *American Educational Research Journal,* 44 (3) pp. 454–459.

Hollingsworth, S. and Sockett, H. (1994). "Positioning Teacher Research in Educational Reform: An Introduction", in *Teacher Research and Educational Reform.* S. Hollingsworth and H. Sockett (Ed.). Chicago: University of Chicago/NSSE.

Hord, S. *Professional Learning Communities: communities of continuous inquiry and improvement.* Austin, Texas: Southwest Educational Development Laboratory.

Hoy, W. & Tarter, J. (2004). Organisational justice in schools: no justice without trust. *International Journal of Educational Management* 18 (4) pp. 250–259.

Huberman, M. (1992). "Teacher Development and Instructional Mastery", in *Understanding Teacher Development.* A. Hargreaves and M. Fullan (Ed.). London: Cassell.

Huberman, M. (1996). "Moving mainstream: taking a closer look at teacher research." *Language Arts* **73**: 124–140.

Independent Schools Teacher Accreditation Authority (2008a). *Classroom/Professional Excellence: NSW Teachers Information Brochure.* Sydney: ISTAA. Available from http:// www.aisnsw.edu.au/Main/ISTAA/tabid/614/Default.aspx, Accessed 20 April 2008.

Independent Schools Teacher Accreditation Authority (2008b). *Experienced Teacher: NSW Teachers Information Brochure.* Sydney: ISTAA. Available from http://www.aisnsw.edu.au/ Main/ISTAA/tabid/614/Default.aspx, Accessed 20 April 2008.

Jenkins, H., Clinton, K., Purushotma, R., Robinson, A. & Weigel, M. (2006). Confronting the Challenges of Participatory Culture: Media Education for the 21ˢᵗ Century. Online article.

Johnson, K. (2007). *Researching with Children: Exploring Children's Place(s) in their Local Primary School.* Unpublished EdD Dissertation. Adelaide: University of South Australia.

Katerndahl, D. & Crabtree, B. (2006). Creating Innovative Research Designs: The 10-Year Methodological Think Tank Case Study. *Annals of Family Medicine,* 4 (September/October) pp 443–449.

Kavaloski, J. (2007). But Then it Got Real. *Creating Equitable Classrooms through Action Research* C. Caro-Bruce, R. Flessner *et al.* Thousand Oaks: Corwin Press.

Keen, A. (2007). *The Cult of the Amateur: How Today's Internet is Killing Our Culture and Assaulting Our Economy.* London: Nicholas Brealey Publishing.

Keka"le, T., & Viitala, R. (2003). Do networks learn? *Journal of Workplace Learning.* 15 (6) pp. 245–247.

Kemmis, S. (1993). "Action Research and Social Movement: A Challenge for Policy Research." *Education Policy Analysis Archives* **1**(1).

Kemmis, S. (2001). "Educational Research and Evaluation: Opening Communicative Space (2000 Radford Lecture)." *Australian Educational Researcher* **28**(1): 1–30.

Kemmis, S. (2006). "Participatory Action Research and the Public Sphere." *Educational Action Research* **14**(4): 459–476.

Kemmis, S. (2007). Participatory Action Research and the Public Sphere. In P. Ponte and B. Smit (Eds.) *The Quality of Practitioner Research.* Rotterdam: Sense Publishers, pp. 9–28.

Kemmis, S. (2008). Passages through Time: How Practice is Prefigures in Practice Architectures. Unpublished manuscript.

Kemmis, S. & Conlan, B. (2006). Towards a new definition of critical participatory action research. Paper presented to the Collaborative Action Research Network (CARN) Conference, Nottingham, Nov. 10–12.

Kemmis, S. and Grundy, S. (1997). "Educational Action Research in Australia: Organizations and Practice", in *International Action Research: A Casebook for Educational Reform.* S. Hollingsworth (Ed.). London: Falmer Press.

Kemmis, S. & Smith, T. (Eds.) (2007). *Enabling Praxis: Challenges for Education.* Rotterdam: Sense Publishers.

Kuhn, R. (2002). Marxist Political Economy in Australia since the mid 1970s'. *Journal of Australian Political Economy,* 50 (December) pp. 107–129.

Labaree, D. (2000). "On the Nature of Teaching and Teacher Education: Difficult Practices that Look Easy." *Journal of Teacher Education* 51(3): 228–233.

Lash, S. (2003). Reflexivity as non-linearity. *Theory, Culture and Society,* 20 (2) pp. 49–57.

Lather, P. (2006). Paradigm proliferation as a good thing to think with: teaching research in education as a wild profusion. *International Journal of Qualitative Studies in Education,* 19 (1) pp. 35–57.

Lee, A., Green, B., et al. (2000). Organisational Knowledge, Professional Practice and the Professional Doctorate at Work. *Research and Knowledge at Work: Perspectives, Case Studies and Innovative Strategies.* J. Garrick and C. Rhodes. London: Routledge: 117–136.

Leonard, D., Becker, R., et al. (2005). "To Prove Myself at the Highest Level: The Benefits of Doctoral Study." *Higher Education Research and Development* 24(2): 135–149.

Levin, B. (2004). Inevitable Tensions in Managing Large-Scale Public Sector Reform. Paper presented at the Advance Institute of Management (AIM) Research Conference, University of Bath, March, 2004.

Lewin, K. (1946). *Resolving Social Conflicts.* New York: Harper and Row.

Lieberman, A. and Miller, L. (1990). "Teacher Development in Professional Practice Schools." *Teachers' College Record* 92(1): 105–122.

Lortie, D. (1975). *Schoolteacher: A Sociological Study.* Chicago: University of Chicago Press.

Loucks-Horsley, S. (1999). *Designing Professional Development for Teachers of Science and Mathematics.* Thousand Oaks, CA: Corwin Press.

Loucks-Horsley, S., Harding, C., et al. (1987). *Continuing to Learn: A Guidebook for Teacher Development.* Andover, MA: Regional Laboratory for Educational Improvement of the Northeast and Islands and National Staff Development Council.

MacBeath, J. & Jardine, S. (1998). I didn't know he was ill–the role and value of the critical friend. *Improving Schools,* 11 (1), pp. 41–47.

MacGilchrist, B., Myers, K. & Reed, J. (2004). *The Intelligent School (2nd Edition).* London: Sage Publications.

Marshall, J. (1984). John Dewey and Educational Research. *Journal of Research and Development in Education,* 17 (3) pp. 66–77.

Marzano, R.J. (2003). *What Works in Schools: Translating Research into Action.* Alexandria, VA: Association for Supervision and Curriculum Development.

McNeil, L. (2002). Private Asset or Public Good: Education and Democracy at the Crossroads. *American Educational Research Journal* 39 (2) pp. 243–248.

Merten, D. (2003). Mixed Methods and the Politics of Human Research: the Transformative-Emancipatory Perspective. In A. Tashakkori & C. Teddlie (Eds.) *Handbook of Mixed Methods in Social and Behavioural Research.* Thousand oaks, CA: Sage Publications.

Meyerson, D. (2008). *Rocking the Boat.* Sydney: McGraw Hill Education, Australia and New Zealand.

Mitra, D. (2004). The Significance of Students: Can Increasing 'Student Voice' in Schools Lead to Gains in Youth Development? In *Teachers College Record* 104(4), April 2004, pp. 651–688.

Mockler, N. (2000). *Making Teacher Learning Count: Building Professionalism at Loreto Normanhurst.* Paper presented to the 4th International Practitioner Research Conference, University of Innsbruck, Austria, September 2000.

Mockler, N. (2001). *Professional Learning Portfolios: A Tool for the Reflective Practitioner.* Paper presented to the Australian Association for Research in Education Annual Conference, University of Notre Dame, Fremantle, December 2001.

Mockler, N. (2002). *Challenging Practice Through Practitioner Inquiry.* Paper presented to the British Educational Research Association Annual Conference, University of Exeter, September 2002.

Mockler, N. (2003). *Improvement Through Inquiry: Evidence Based Practice and School Improvement.* Paper presented to the International Congress for School Effectiveness and Improvement, Sydney, January 2003.

Mockler, N. (2005). "Trans/Forming Teachers: New Professional Learning and Transformative Teacher Professionalism." *Journal of In-service Education* 31(4): 733–746.

Mockler, N. (2007). Ethics in practitioner research: Dilemmas from the field. In A. Campbell and S. Groundwater-Smith (Eds.) *An Ethical Approach to Practitioner Research.* London: Routledge, pp. 88–98.

Mockler, N. (2008). *Beyond 'What Works': Teachers and the Politics of Identity.* Sydney: The University of Sydney. Unpublished PhD Thesis.

Mockler, N. and Groundwater-Smith, S. (2009, forthcoming). "From Lesson Study to Learning Study: Side-by-Side Professional Learning in the Classroom", in A. Campbell and S. Groundwater-Smith (Eds), *Connecting Inquiry and Professional Learning in Education: Joining the Dots.* Abingdon: Routledge.

Mockler, N. and Sachs, J. (2002). "A Crisis of Identity? Teacher Professional Identity and the Role of Evidence Based Practice". Paper presented to the Australian Association for Educational Research Annual Conference, University of Queensland, December 2002.

Mockler, N., Schutz, H. and Vecchiet, S. (2005). "Practitioner Inquiry for Professional Learning: Possibilities, Capabilities and Accountabilities". Paper presented to the PRAR/CARN Conference, Utrecht, The Netherlands, November 2005.

Muncey, D. & McQuillan, P. (1996). *Reform and Resistance in Schools and Classrooms: An Ethnographic View of the Coalition of Essential Schools.* New Haven, Yale University Press.

Munns, G., Zammit, K. & Woodward, H. (2006). Reflections from the Riot Zone: The Fair Go Project and Student Engagement in a Besieged Community. Paper presented at the Annual Conference of the Australian Association for Research in Education, Adelaide, December.

Needham, K. (2006). Zen and the art of school improvement: a case study of using students as researchers into their own learning. Paper presented to the joint Collaborative Action Research Network/Practitioner Research Conference. Utrecht, November.

Newman, M. (2006). *Teaching Defiance: Stories and Strategies for Activist Educators.* San Francisco: Jossey Bass.

Noden, C. & Bruce, D. (Eds.) *Cracking the Concrete: David Jackson in Conversation with Madeline Church.* Nottingham: National College of School Leadership.

Noffke, S. (1994). "Action Research: towards the next generation." *Educational Action Research* 2(1): 9–12.

Noffke, S. (1997). "Themes and tensions in US action research: Towards historical analysis", in *International Action Research: A casebook for Educational Reform.* S. Hollingsworth (Ed.). London: Falmer.

Nonaka, I. and Takeuchi, H. (1995). *The Knowledge-Creating Company.* Oxford: Oxford University Press.

Nowotny, H., Scott, P. & Gibbons, M. (2001). Re-Thinking Science: Knowledge and the Public in an Age of Uncertainty. Cambridge: Polity Press.

Nowotny, H., Scott, P. & Gibbons, H. (2003). Mode 2 Revisited: The New Production of Knowledge. *Minerva,* 41, pp. 179–194.

Nussbaum, M. (2001). The enduring significance of John Rawls. *The Chronicle of Higher Education,* July 20, 2001. http://chronicle.com/free/v47/i45/45b00701.htm Accessed 17th January, 2008.

Orwell, G. (1946). Politics and the English Language http://ebooks.adelaide.edu.au/o/orwell/george/o79e/part42.html Accessed 9th July, 2008

Pfeffer, J. & Sutton, R. (2000). *The Knowing-doing Gap*. Boston: Harvard Business School Press.

Power, M. (1999). *The Audit Society: Rituals of Verification*. Oxford: Oxford University Press.

Power, M. (2004). *The Risk Management of Everything: Rethinking the Politics of Uncertainty*. London: DEMOS.

Power, M. (2007). *Organized Uncertainty: Designing a World of Risk Management*. Oxford: Oxford University Press.

Raymond, L. (2001). Student Involvement in School Improvement; from Data Source to Significant Voice. *Forum* 43 (2) pp. 58–61.

Reckwitz, A. (2002). Toward a Theory of Social Practice. *European Journal of Social Theory* 5 (2) pp. 243–263.

Richards, S. (2007). What Strategies Can I Incorporate So That English Language Learners in My Classroom Will Better Understand Oral Directions? *Creating Equitable Classrooms through Action Research* C. Caro-Bruce, R. Flessner *et al.* Thousand Oaks: Corwin Press.

Rose, J. (2006). *Independent Review of the Teaching of Early Reading*. London: Department of Education and Skills (DES).

Rudduck, J. (2006). "Student Voice, Student Engagement and School Reform." In D. Thiessen and A. Cook-Sather (Eds) *International Handbook of Student Experience in Elementary and Secondary School*. Amsterdam: Springer. pp.587–610.

Rudduck, J. and Flutter, J. (2004). *How to Improve your School: Giving Students a Voice*. New York and London: Continuum.

Rudduck, J. and Hopkins, D. (1985). *Research as a Basis for Teaching: Readings from the Work of Lawrence Stenhouse*. London: Heinemann.

Rudduck, J. & McIntyre, D. (2007). *Improving Learning through Consulting Pupils*. London: Routledge

Sabar, N. (2004). From Heaven to Reality through Crisis: Novice Teachers as Migrants. *Teaching and Teacher Education*, 20 (2) pp. 145–161.

Sachs, J. (1997). "Renewing teacher professionalism through innovative links." *Educational Action Research* 5(3): 449–462.

Sachs, J. (1999). "Using teacher research as a basis for professional renewal." *Journal of Inservice Education* 25(1): 39–53.

Sachs, J. (2000). "The Activist Professional." *Journal of Educational Change* 1: 77–95.

Sachs, J. (2001). "Learning to be a Teacher: Teacher Education and the Development of Professional Identity." *Paper presented to the ISATT Conference, Faro Portugal, 21–25 September 2001*.

Sachs, J. (2003a). "Teacher professional Standards: Controlling or Developing Teachers." *Teachers and Teaching: Theory and Practice* 9(2): 175–186.

Sachs, J. (2003b). *The Activist Teaching Profession*. Buckingham: Open University Press.

Sachs, J. (2007). Learning to Improve or Improving Learning: The Dilemma of Teacher Continuing Professional Development. Keynote Address presented to the ICSEI Conference, Slovenia, 3rd–6th January.

Sachs, J. & Mellor, L. (2003) Child Panic and Child Protection Policy: A Critical Examination of Policies from NSW and Queensland. Paper presented to the joint AARE/NZARE Annual Conference, Auckland.

Sarason, S. (1971). *The Culture of the School and the Problem of Change*. Boston: Allyn and Bacon.

Sarason, S. (1996). *Revisiting The Culture of the School and the Problem of Change*. New York: Teachers' College Press.

Saunders, L. (2004). Evidence-led professional creativity, *Educational Action Research Journal*, 12 (1) pp. 163–166.

Schatzki, T. (2005). Peripheral Vision: The Sites of Organisations. *Organisation Studies* 26 (3) pp. 465–484.

Schleicher, A. (2007). Literacy Skills in the Information Age. Paper presented to the 15th European Conference on Reading, Humboldt University.

Schon, D.A. (1983). *The Reflective Practitioner*. New York: Basic Books.

Seddon, T., Billett, S. & Clemans, A. (2005). Navigating social partnerships: Central agencies - local networks. *British Journal of Sociology of Education,* 26 (5) pp. 567–584.

Senge, P. (1992). *The Fifth Discipline: The Art and Practice of the Learning Organisation.* New York: Doubleday.

Senge, P., Cambron-McCabe, N., et al. (2000). *Schools That Learn.* London: Nicholas Brealey.

Shager, E. (2007). Been There, Done That: Student Inquiry About High School Dropouts. *Creating Equitable Classrooms through Action Research* C. Caro-Bruce, R. Flessner et al. Thousand Oaks: Corwin Press.

Shavelson, R. & Towne L. (Eds.) (2002). *Scientific Research in Education.* Washington, DC: National Research Council.

Siemens, G. 2006. *Knowing Knowledge.* Retrieved 18th July, 2007 from http://knowingknowledge. com/.

Singh, M. (2007). A Sound Research Base for Beginning Teacher Education. *Asia Pacific Journal of Teacher Education.* 35 (4) pp. 333–349.

Sizer, T. (1984). *Horace's Compromise: The Dilemma of the American High School.* Boston: Mariner Books (Houghton Mifflin).

Snyder, I. (2008). *The Literacy Wars, Why Teaching Children to Read and Write is a Battleground in Australia.* Sydney: Allen & Unwin.

Sockett, H. (1993). *The Moral Basis for Teacher Professionalism.* New York: Teachers College Press.

Somekh, B. (1994). "Inhabiting each other's castles: towards knowledge and mutual growth through collaboration." *Educational Action Research* 2(2): 357–381.

Stenhouse, L. (1979a). Research as a Basis for Teaching. Inaugural Lecture University of East Anglia. In Stenhouse, L. (1983) *Authority, Education and Emancipation.* London: Heinemann Educational Books.

Stenhouse, L. (1979b). "The problems of standards in illuminative research." *Scottish Educational Review* 11(1).

Stenhouse, L. (1980). "The Study of Samples and the Study of Cases." *British Educational Research Journal* 6(1): 1–6.

Stenhouse, L. (1981). "What counts as research?" *British Journal of Educational Studies* 29(2).

Stenhouse, L. (1983). *Toward a Vernacular Humanism: Authority, Education and Emancipation.* London: Heinemann.

Stenhouse, L. (1985a). "Can research improve teaching?" in *Research as a Basis for Teaching: Readings from the Work of Lawrence Stenhouse.* J. Rudduck and D. Hopkins (Ed.). London: Heinemann Press.

Stenhouse, L. (1985b). "Using research means doing research", in *Research as a Basis for Teaching.* J. Rudduck and D. Hopkins (Ed.). London: Heinemann.

Stenhouse, L. (1985c). "Action research and the teacher's responsibility for the educational process", in *Research as a Basis for Teaching: Readings from the Work of Lawrence Stenhouse.* J. Rudduck and D. Hopkins (Ed.). London: Heinemann Press.

Stoll, J. (2005). Developing Professional Learning Communities: Messages for Learning Networks. In D. Aspin et al *International Perspectives on Networked Learning.* Nottingham: National College of School Leadership. Pp. 10–14.

Stoll, L., Bolam, R., McMahon, A., Wallace, M. and Thomas, S. (2006). Professional Learning Communities: A Review of the Literature. *Journal of Educational Change,*7, pp. 221– 258.

Stott, A. Jopling, M. & Kilcher, A. (2006). How do School-to-School networks work. Nottingham: National College of School Leadership.

Strathern, M., Ed. (2000). *Audit Cultures.* London: Routledge.

Swaffield, S. (2007). Light touch critical friendship. *Improving Schools.* 10 (3) pp. 205–219.

Swaffield, S. & MacBeath, J. (2005). School self-evaluation and the role of the critical friend. *Cambridge Journal of Education,* 35 (2) pp. 239–252.

Thomson, P. & Gunter, H. (2007). The Methodology of Students-as-Researchers: Valuing and using experience and expertise to develop methods. *Discourse* 28 (3) pp. 327–342.

USDOE (2004). *Fact Sheet: New No Child Left Behind Flexibility: Highly Qualified Teachers.* Washington, DC: US Department of Education.

Valenti, M. (2002). Creating the Classroom of the Future. *Educause,* September/October.

Van Galen, J. (2004). Seeing classes: Toward a broadened research agenda for critical qualitative researchers. *International Journal of Qualitative Studies in Education,* 17 (5) pp. 663–684.

Warren Little, J. (1993). "Teachers' Professional Development in a Climate of Educational Reform." *Educational Evaluation and Policy Analysis* **15**(2): 129–151.

Warren Little, J. (2002). Locating learning in teachers' communities of practice: Opening up problems of analysis in records of everyday work. *Teaching and Teacher Education.* 18 pp. 917–946.

Watson, D. (2003). *Death Sentence: The Decay of Public Language.* Sydney: Random House.

Watson, D. (2004). *Watson's Dictionary of Weasel Words.* Sydney: Random House.

Wenger, E. (1998). *Communities of Practice: Learning, Meaning and Identity.* Cambridge: Cambridge University Press.

Williams, R. (1983). *The Year 2000.* New York: Pantheon Books.

Yeatman, A. and Sachs, J. (1995). *Making the Links: A Formative Evaluation of the First Year of the Innovative Links Between Schools and Universities project for Teacher Professional Development.* Murdoch: Murdoch University.

Young, J. (2005). On Insiders (Emic) and Outsiders (Etic): Views of Self and Othering. *Systemic Practice and Action Research,* 18 (2) pp. 151–162.

Zevernbergen, R. & Zevernbergen, K. (2007). Millenials Come to School. In S. Knipe (Ed.) *Middle Years Schooling: Reframing Adolescence.* Sydney: Pearson, pp. 23–36.

Author Index

Subject Index

Lightning Source UK Ltd.
Milton Keynes UK
28 September 2009

144293UK00006B/8/P